"In the Family Project Focus on the Family has given us a unique resource to strengthen, empower and support the family as the Creator designed it to be. This project is sure to give you the tools you need to build the family God desires you to have."

—DR. TONY EVANS
President, The Urban Alternative
Senior Pastor, Oak Cliff Bible Fellowship

"Healthy, stable families are one of society's most precious resources. We need to do everything we can to protect and promote them. The Family Project has a timely message for the Church, and for the culture at large."

—ANDY STANLEY
Senior Pastor, North Point Ministries

"When you look at a family, you're looking at a God-designed picture of the gospel. This has profound implications for the Church and for society. The Family Project explores the theology of the family in an informative and accessible manner that lends itself to small group discussion. I highly recommend it!"

—DR. RUSSELL D. MOORE
President, Southern Baptist Ethics and Religious
Liberty Commission

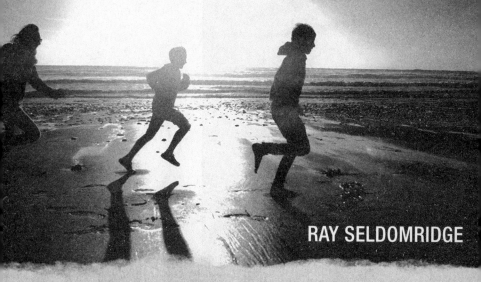

RAY SELDOMRIDGE

The Family project™ Devotional

REFLECTING GOD'S DESIGN IN YOUR HOME

TYNDALE HOUSE PUBLISHERS, INC.
CAROL STREAM, ILLINOIS

The Family Project Devotional
© 2014 Focus on the Family

A Focus on the Family book published by Tyndale House Publishers, Inc., Carol Stream, Illinois 60188

Focus on the Family, the accompanying logo and design, and The Family Project are trademarks of Focus on the Family, 8605 Explorer Drive, Colorado Springs, CO 80920.

Cataloging-in-Publication Data for this book is available by contacting the Library of Congress.

Reference to websites does not imply endorsement of those sites in their entirety. Availability of websites and pages is subject to change without notice.

Printed in the United States of America
1   2   3   4   5   6   7   8   9 /19   18   17   16   15   14

Contents

Foreword

When our team here at Focus on the Family first started working on *The Family Project*, we struggled to adequately define the scope of this endeavor. Is it primarily a work of theology—an academic exercise in the biblical principles that define and outline the family? Or is it more of a tool for families—a user-friendly assortment of practical helps that allows them to distill those big biblical concepts into everyday applications?

As the project unfolded, we realized that *The Family Project* needed to be *both* of those things: a much-needed reintroduction to the biblical concept of the family for those living in a postmodern world, and a practical tool to inspire and equip families to be the best they can be.

Nowhere are these two goals more fully realized than in the book you're now holding, *The Family Project Devotional*. Within the pages that follow, you'll delve deep into Scripture to discover the DNA of God's design for the family. You'll celebrate the fact that the historical institution of the family is a direct reflection of the Creator himself.

But you'll also encounter a wealth of useful, practical tips to help you discover how those timeless theological principles relate directly to *you* and to *your family*—right now, at this moment in history. You'll find encouraging and inspirational tips to not only strengthen your own family, but to make a dramatic impact on other families in your sphere of influence, and on the world around you.

May God bless you and your loved ones as you celebrate His design in *The Family Project Devotional*.

—Jim Daly
May 2014

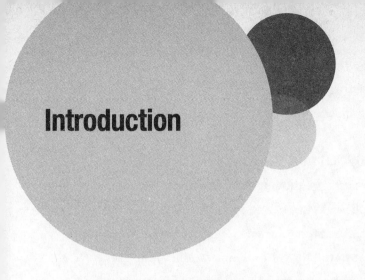

Introduction

This book contains 52 devotional themes, one for every week in the year. Within each week, we provide daily Scripture readings.

The rationale behind the choice of most topics is that the Bible, particularly the New Testament, gives numerous exhortations to Christians on what they should do for and with one another. Of course, these "one anothers" apply wherever two or more believers are gathered. But the place that offers the best opportunity for significant Christian relationships is the home. What happens in the family not only affects every member, but it also impacts the larger church of which the family is a part. And that will determine what sort of light we're able to shine into our dark world.

Specifically, here's what this book offers for each week:

First, the topic and a subtitle to explain it a bit more. You'll find that some topics overlap or are distinct only in subtle ways. Also, some deal with other aspects of family life; not all are derived from the "one anothers." Then:

1 **Opening Prayer** to begin the day with the Lord and to zero in on the topic for the week.

2 **Daily Scripture Reading,** often consisting of several passages, though most of them are short. On some weeks, we've also suggested additional readings. And we've chosen one passage each week to print in full for your memorization. Some of the assigned readings in this book will reoccur, since the same Bible passage can touch upon multiple topics.

3 **Activity of the Day,** which most often is a series of questions related to the Scripture readings for that day. Some blank lines have been provided so that you can jot down answers or record notes for further reflection. Do not feel that you have to answer every question; we've provided more than one so you can pick the questions that strike a chord with you.

Occasionally the activity for the day is, instead of questions, a suggested assignment for the whole family.

4 **Conclusion** to summarize the main teachings of the week.

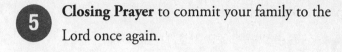 **Closing Prayer** to commit your family to the Lord once again.

This devotional was written for an individual reader or a married couple. But since it's all about family, we've indicated a few places where you can involve your children if you so choose. May you all, together, hear God's voice through this yearlong tour of His Word.

In the Beginning

The family is God's idea.

1 OPENING PRAYER

Lord, reveal to us what kind of people You have made us to be. Help us understand Your basic design for all of humanity, so we may live in a way that pleases You. In Jesus's name. Amen.

2 SCRIPTURE READING

Monday	GENESIS 1:26-28
Tuesday	GENESIS 2:18-25
Wednesday	GENESIS 4:1-2
Thursday	GENESIS 12:1-3
Friday	PSALM 128:3-4
Saturday	MARK 10:7-9
Sunday	EPHESIANS 3:14-16

FEATURED SCRIPTURE

I bow my knees before the Father, from whom every family in heaven and on earth is named, that according to the riches of his glory he may grant you to be strengthened with power through his Spirit in your inner being. —EPHESIANS 3:14-16

3 ACTIVITY OF THE DAY

Monday

Answer this: Have you ever stopped and marveled at the existence of the family, or have you always just taken it for granted, like the air you breathe? Why?

_____

_____

_____

_____

Tuesday

What would your life be like without a family? How might society function without families?

_____

_____

_____

_____

Wednesday

Ask your spouse what's the first thing that comes to mind when recalling the family that he or she was raised in. Then share about your own family. Pray together for your parents and siblings. (If unmarried, do this with a close friend.)

Thursday

Based on the book of Genesis, how would you define a family?

_____

_____

_____

_____

Friday

At dinner, share with your spouse and/or children what you're learning or thinking about God's invention called the family.

Saturday

What did Jesus say about marriage? About divorce? Why?

_____

_____

_____

_____

Sunday

Memorize this week's featured Bible passage or your favorite portion from one of the other readings.

4 CONCLUSION

God is one, yet He is also a community of three Persons. We, too, are individuals, but we were meant to live in relationship to others. By God's design, the primary way we do that is the family, where a man and woman, together with their children, form the building block on which all of society is based. Without strong, lasting families, nothing in life can hold together.

5 CLOSING PRAYER

Talk to God alone or together about your family, friends, church, and community, as well as about what He is saying to you today through His Word. Then conclude with this:

> *Father, thank You for families. Teach us to act rightly toward all members of our own family, and show us how to reach out to those who have no family at all. Amen.*

We Need One Another

Families aren't just a nice idea—they're necessary.

1 OPENING PRAYER

Dear Lord, forgive us for thinking that we can go through life on our own power. Show us more and more why You placed us in families for mutual support. Amen.

2 SCRIPTURE READING

Monday	ECCLESIASTES 4:9-12
Tuesday	ROMANS 12:4-8
Wednesday	PROVERBS 27:17
Thursday	ROMANS 1:11-12
Friday	1 CORINTHIANS 12:14-25
Saturday	2 PETER 1:5-8
Sunday	EPHESIANS 4:15-16

See also GENESIS 2:18-24; 4:9-10; ISAIAH 41:6-7; LUKE 6:41-42; ROMANS 14:14-20; 1 CORINTHIANS 12:4-11; HEBREWS 10:24-25; 1 JOHN 3:16-18

3 ACTIVITY OF THE DAY

Monday

Answer this: In biblical times, people thought much more about "we"
than "I." In what ways has Western culture's emphasis on "me" col-
ored your outlook on the family? On the church?

_____

_____

_____

_____

Tuesday

In a fun family discussion over a meal, let everyone say what they are
best at, what "gift" they offer that the rest of the family needs. It could
be a skill, or it might be a personality trait, like "always being positive."
Let others provide helpful feedback after each family member speaks.

Wednesday

"Iron sharpens iron." Who in your life provides you with that kind of
support?

_____

_____

_____

_____

Thursday

How much do you really *need* your spouse? Each of your children?
Are you able to develop a godly character without others knowing
(and working with you on) your innermost struggles and weaknesses?
Explain.

_____

_____

_____

_____

Friday

Is Scripture saying that things work out much better when we join
together, or that we simply can't do much of anything without one
another? Which is closer to the truth? Why?

_____

_____

_____

_____

Saturday

Pick a family activity or chore that you can accomplish only if you all pitch in and do it together. Then grab a dessert and talk about the day's work.

Sunday

Memorize this week's featured Bible passage or your favorite portion from one of the other readings.

4 CONCLUSION

Your family is more than a collection of individuals living under one roof. It's a body that thrives only when all parts are working together as a whole. But in a culture driven by an emphasis on the individual, this biblical truth is almost unimaginable. We *need* one another. Our lives are defined and made meaningful only in relationship to others.

5 CLOSING PRAYER

Talk to God alone or together about your family, friends, church, and community, as well as about what He is saying to you today through His Word. Then conclude with this:

> *Lord, forgive us when we think or say, "I have no real need*
> *for that family (or church) member." As we work through*
> *this devotional guide, show us what sort of relationships*
> *You desire us to have, so that together we can grow up into*
> *You and become more fruitful in our faith. Amen.*

A Family That Worships

The church in your house

1 OPENING PRAYER

Father, we honor You this day. Make Your presence known as we look into Your Scriptures to discover what it means to worship You. In Jesus's name. Amen.

2 SCRIPTURE READING

Monday	DEUTERONOMY 16:11
Tuesday	JOHN 4:19-24
Wednesday	1 CORINTHIANS 16:19
Thursday	1 PETER 2:4-5
Friday	COLOSSIANS 3:15-17
Saturday	EPHESIANS 2:19-22
Sunday	HEBREWS 12:28

See also ROMANS 16:3-5; EPHESIANS 5:18-20; 1 THESSALONIANS 5:16-18

FEATURED SCRIPTURE

Whatever you do, in word or deed, do everything in the name of the Lord Jesus, giving thanks to God the Father through him. —COLOSSIANS 3:17

3 ACTIVITY OF THE DAY

Monday

When and where do you worship the Lord? Why just these times and places?

_____

_____

_____

_____

_____

Tuesday

Discuss as a family what sort of worship is most meaningful to each of you. What kind of worship does God seek?

_____

_____

_____

Wednesday

Does your family gather for worship together at home? Why or why not? If such worship would feel awkward, talk about the reasons for that.

_____

_____

_____

_____

_____

Thursday

As an exercise in family worship, spend at least five minutes together thanking God for one thing after another, big or small. Let it go on as long as people think of more things to add.

Friday

Besides singing and praying, what activities do you also consider to be worship? When you do them, are you consciously offering yourself up to God? Why or why not?

_____

_____

_____

_____

Saturday

Is your family a "dwelling place for God"? What changes would make it even more so?

_____

_____

_____

_____

Sunday

Memorize this week's featured Bible passage or your favorite portion from one of the other readings.

4 CONCLUSION

Wherever Christians gather, in a spacious sanctuary or cozy kitchen, Jesus is there. And the first response to Jesus is always worship. So we should never feel that "going to church" is the only way to worship God. Nor should we limit worship to singing and the study of His Word. As the apostle Paul said, *everything* we do can be an act of worship.

5 CLOSING PRAYER

Talk to God alone or together about your family, friends, church, and community, as well as about what He is saying to you today through His Word. Then conclude with this:

> *Lord, make our home a dwelling place for You. May*
> *we as a family always and everywhere offer You*
> *reverent and acceptable worship. Amen.*

At Home with Gratitude

*"We thank thee, Lord,
for happy hearts . . ."*

1 OPENING PRAYER

Father, show us the way to genuine happiness through thanksgiving,
so that we might be content in You, and You might be pleased by us.
In Jesus's name. Amen.

2 SCRIPTURE READING

Monday	PSALM 92:1-4; 95:1-7; 100:1-5
Tuesday	LUKE 17:12-19
Wednesday	COLOSSIANS 1:11-14; 4:2
Thursday	PHILIPPIANS 4:4-7; 1 THESSALONIANS 5:16-18
Friday	PSALM 105:1-4
Saturday	JOHN 15:11; 17:13; EPHESIANS 5:18-20
Sunday	COLOSSIANS 2:6-7

See also 1 CHRONICLES 16:7-11; PSALM 50:14; 2 TIMOTHY 3:2

FEATURED SCRIPTURE

*Therefore, as you received Christ Jesus the Lord, so walk in him, rooted
and built up in him and established in the faith, just as you were taught,
abounding in thanksgiving.* —COLOSSIANS 2:6-7

3 ACTIVITY OF THE DAY

Monday

List some things that the Bible says we should be thankful for. Why is it "good to give thanks to the Lord," to sing praises to His name? Why does the Lord want us not just to serve Him, but to serve Him "with gladness"?

_____

_____

_____

_____

Tuesday

When do you personally make it a point to give thanks to God? How often are you like the lepers who forgot? What do you want to do about it?

_____

_____

_____

_____

Wednesday

Answer one or more of the following: Is your family a joyful family? If not, why? What spoils your joy at home? What enhances it? And who are the happiest people in your family? Who are the least happy? What might older people learn from the young?

_____

_____

_____

_____

Thursday

Identify some people in your life who seem most content, perhaps even jovial or exuberant. What makes them that way? Is it because everything is going well for them, or are they also grateful in the midst of pain and tragedy? Under what circumstances is joy inappropriate or not expected?

_____

_____

_____

_____

Friday

As a family, brainstorm and write down (on a dry-erase board or poster) everything you'd like to thank God for. If that's too big of a list, focus on what to thank Him for from just the past month or even week.

Saturday

What is the source of our joy? Is God himself a happy God, joyful even while sorrowing over the world's sin? What do today's Bible passages tell us?

Sunday

Memorize this week's featured Bible passage or your favorite portion from one of the other readings.

4 CONCLUSION

Gratitude is a key theme in the Bible. Since we owe much to our loving and joyous heavenly Father, Christian families should abound in thanksgiving at all times, even in the midst of trials. His creation of the world, His amazing acts to save us, and His own glorious character deserve endless praise. Any home that demonstrates such gratitude is a powerful witness to those who don't know Him.

5 CLOSING PRAYER

Talk to God alone or together about your family, friends, church, and community, as well as about what He is saying to you today through His Word. Then conclude with this:

Lord, erase all ingratitude from our hearts and make us people who never cease to be happy in You. For everything You have done for us, we offer eternal thanks. In Jesus's name. Amen.

Follow and Serve the Lord

Abraham and Moses knew literally what it meant to follow the Lord.

1 OPENING PRAYER

Lord, You have called us to follow in Your footsteps. Show us this week what that means and how we can do it better. Amen.

2 SCRIPTURE READING

Monday	DEUTERONOMY 10:12-13
Tuesday	JOHN 10:27-28
Wednesday	JOHN 12:25-26
Thursday	EPHESIANS 5:8-10, 15-17
Friday	PHILIPPIANS 1:27-28
Saturday	COLOSSIANS 1:9-14
Sunday	ROMANS 8:35-39; 1 PETER 2:21

See also LUKE 4:8; 1 CORINTHIANS 4:1; PHILIPPIANS 2:14-15

FEATURED SCRIPTURE

"Whoever loves his life loses it, and whoever hates his life in this world will keep it for eternal life. If anyone serves me, he must follow me; and where I am, there will my servant be also. If anyone serves me, the Father will honor him." —JOHN 12:25-26

3 ACTIVITY OF THE DAY

Monday

How might *following* the Lord and *serving* Him go hand in hand?

_____

_____

_____

_____

Tuesday

Did you follow Jesus to get where you are today? By what means does He make His voice known to you?

_____

_____

_____

_____

Wednesday

What did Jesus mean by "hating" one's life in order to serve Him instead? How are you doing that?

_____

_____

_____

_____

Thursday

When we decide to follow the Lord, what sort of walking does that require? Describe in your own words what the Lord is looking for in His followers.

_____

_____

_____

_____

Friday

Identify how, as a family, you can help one another follow the Lord on some specific assignment He has given you individually.

_____

_____

_____

_____

Saturday

At dinnertime or on an outing, discuss whether the Lord is calling you *as a family* to serve Him in some specific way. What's going on in your extended family, church, or community that needs your family's participation?

_____

_____

_____

Sunday

Following Jesus can sometimes be difficult and costly. If you're not accustomed to suffering for your faith, how prepared are you for this possibility in the days to come? What causes us sometimes to feel separated from our leader, Jesus?

_____

_____

_____

_____

4 CONCLUSION

Every wise hiker knows to take a companion when wandering into the wild, since there is safety and strength in numbers. So in following Jesus, isn't that what families are for? Only together can we effectively serve the Lord and endure hardships along the way.

5 CLOSING PRAYER

Talk to God alone or together about your family, friends, church, and community, as well as about what He is saying to you today through His Word. Then conclude with this:

> *Jesus, take our hands and lead us where You want us to go.*
> *May we as a family recognize Your voice and obediently*
> *follow, bearing fruit in every good work. Amen.*

With One Voice

Praying together is not just something to do at a church meeting or worship service.

1 OPENING PRAYER

O Lord, You have saved us and brought us into a family of believers, often including our own natural family, with whom to worship and serve You. Teach us how You would have us pray together. Amen.

2 SCRIPTURE READING

Monday	MATTHEW 18:19-20
Tuesday	ACTS 1:14; 2:42
Wednesday	ACTS 12:5-17
Thursday	EPHESIANS 5:18-21
Friday	PHILIPPIANS 4:5-7
Saturday	NEHEMIAH 9 (all)
Sunday	1 PETER 3:7

See also MATTHEW 6:9-13; ACTS 4:23-31; COLOSSIANS 4:2-4

The Lord is at hand; do not be anxious about anything, but in every-thing by prayer and supplication with thanksgiving let your requests be made known to God. And the peace of God, which surpasses all understanding, will guard your hearts and your minds in Christ Jesus. —Philippians 4:5-7

3 ACTIVITY OF THE DAY

Monday

Do you pray together as a family? Why or why not? What makes praying together difficult in your home? List some obstacles.

_____

_____

_____

Tuesday

What is your family "devoted to" from day to day? If necessary, how might you change your family's focus?

_____

_____

_____

Wednesday

Read today's exciting (and somewhat comedic) Bible passage aloud to your family. Then discuss: Have you ever prayed for something as a family and then been shocked that God actually heard and answered the prayer? Share examples.

_____

_____

_____

Thursday

Is there a place for singing (which is really just putting prayers to music) in your family? If that sounds crazy, should it? Give it a try, perhaps singing along with one of your kids' favorite songs or praise albums. It's okay to laugh when trying this out for the first time.

_____

_____

_____

Friday

What do you do when your whole family is anxious about something, whether it's a family member's health, a parent getting laid off from a job, etc.?

_____

_____

_____

Saturday

What place is there in your family for longer prayers that review where God has led you all together over the years? You might try doing this conversationally, in which everyone limits prayers to just a sentence or two at a time.

_____

_____

_____

Sunday

Memorize this week's featured Bible passage or your favorite portion from one of the other readings.

4 CONCLUSION

Everyone agrees that Christians are called to worship and pray together regularly. Whether in a corporate service, Bible study group, or gathering of two friends, talking and listening to God is often an important feature. But where is such joint prayer more appropriate than in a Christian marriage and family?

5 CLOSING PRAYER

Talk to God alone or together about your family, friends, church, and community, as well as about what He is saying to you today through His Word. Then conclude with this:

> *Father, You have told us to be anxious for nothing, but in everything to trust You and to rest in Your peace. Help us always to come before You—when we are alone, when we are with friends or family, and when we are in a great congregation—so that we truly learn to pray without ceasing. For Your glory. Amen.*

Sweeter Than Honey

Is your family obsessed with the Word of God?

WEEK 7

1 OPENING PRAYER

Lord, thank You for leading us out of darkness and revealing to us the truth about Yourself and the world You created. Help us to grasp all that You have brought to light. Amen.

2 SCRIPTURE READING

Monday	Deuteronomy 6:4-9
Tuesday	Psalm 119:97-105
Wednesday	Matthew 4:4; 22:37-38
Thursday	Romans 12:1-2
Friday	1 Corinthians 2:6-16
Saturday	2 Peter 3:14-18
Sunday	2 Timothy 3:16; Hebrews 4:12

See also Deuteronomy 4:8-10; 17:18-20; Psalm 1:1-3; Proverbs 2:1-15; John 8:31-32; Acts 17:10-12; Galatians 1:6-9; 2 Timothy 2:7

Do not be conformed to this world, but be transformed by the renewal of your mind, that by testing you may discern what is the will of God, what is good and acceptable and perfect. —ROMANS 12:2

3 ACTIVITY OF THE DAY

Monday

What would it be like to have God's words *always* on your heart and mind? To what extent does Deuteronomy 6:7-9 describe your family?

_____

_____

_____

_____

Tuesday

Do God's words taste "sweeter than honey" to you? Why or why not? How does *knowing* God's words relate to *obeying* God's words?

_____

_____

_____

_____

Wednesday

As a family, discuss what it means to love God "with all your mind." What are some ways you can do that together?

Thursday

How can your family avoid being conformed to the world? Rate how well you and your loved ones are doing at being *in* the world but not *of* it. How can you help one another discern what is right and good?

Friday

How much of coming to know God and His revealed truth is something we can do by our own efforts? How else does it happen?

Saturday

What kind of education are you providing for your children so they will understand Scripture rightly and thoroughly, and won't be carried away by the world's lies?

Sunday

Memorize this week's featured Bible passage or your favorite portion from one of the other readings.

4 CONCLUSION

No matter the topic of the day at your family's dinner table, it should always lead back to the Word of God. Living in a Christian home can be the ultimate educational experience for your children, as they learn together to wrestle with and savor the truths revealed in Scripture. The goal is to cooperate with the Holy Spirit in having our minds—our outlook on *every* aspect of life—transformed into the mind of Christ.

5 CLOSING PRAYER

Talk to God alone or together about your family, friends, church, and community, as well as about what He is saying to you today through His Word. Then conclude with this:

> *Jesus, teach us to abide in You, and to live by every word that comes from Your mouth. By Your Spirit, lead us into all understanding, and thereby into an obedience that pleases You. Amen.*

Love—Family Style

Nothing matters more than love.

1 OPENING PRAYER

Holy Spirit, teach us how to love one another as You have loved us.
Amen.

2 SCRIPTURE READING

Monday	EPHESIANS 3:17-19; 1 JOHN 4:11, 19
Tuesday	1 CORINTHIANS 13:1-7, 13
Wednesday	PHILIPPIANS 2:1-2; COLOSSIANS 3:12-14
Thursday	1 PETER 3:8-9
Friday	PROVERBS 10:12; 1 PETER 1:22-23; 4:8
Saturday	PHILIPPIANS 1:9-11; 1 THESSALONIANS 3:12-13
Sunday	1 THESSALONIANS 4:9-10; HEBREWS 10:24-25

See also LUKE 6:36; GALATIANS 5:13-15; EPHESIANS 5:1-2;
COLOSSIANS 2:1-3

FEATURED SCRIPTURE

May the Lord make you increase and abound in love for one another and for all, as we do for you, so that he may establish your hearts blameless in holiness before our God and Father, at the coming of our Lord Jesus with all his saints. —1 THESSALONIANS 3:12-13

3 ACTIVITY OF THE DAY

Monday

How does being "rooted and grounded" in God's love enable us to love one another? What's the most effective way to become a more loving person (or family)?

_____

_____

_____

_____

Tuesday

Does love for one another dominate your marriage and your family life? To the degree you would like? Explain. What sorts of things hinder you from loving one another more consistently?

_____

_____

_____

_____

Wednesday

How does your family show compassion and sympathy when one family member is hurting? Do your children treat each other with love? What more can you do to achieve "perfect harmony" in your home?

_____

_____

_____

Thursday

At mealtime, start with the youngest family member and have everyone say something that sincerely "blesses" him or her. Then move to the next family member and do the same, until everyone has been blessed by every member.

Friday

Does love come easily? What must you do in your family to love one another "earnestly"? How does love "cover" other people's sins?

_____

_____

_____

Saturday

What is the ultimate purpose behind our loving one another? How does our love for others, in and beyond the family, bring glory to God?

_____

_____

_____

_____

Sunday

How do you learn to love one another? What must you do in your family to encourage such loving behavior?

_____

_____

_____

4 CONCLUSION

The preeminent mark of the Christian family should be love. Various manifestations of this love are addressed throughout this devotional guide. Our love for one another originates from God's love for us even while we were most unlovable. And if we abound in this love, we ultimately will come to reflect God's own character, bringing glory to His name in all the world.

5 CLOSING PRAYER

Talk to God alone or together about your family, friends, church, and community, as well as about what He is saying to you today through His Word. Then conclude with this:

> *Lord, we love because You first loved us. Open our*
> *eyes to the height and depth of Your love, so that*
> *we may learn to love one another in the same way.*
> *Make us imitators of You. In Jesus's name. Amen.*

Good Husbands

*How to be the man
God intended*

1 OPENING PRAYER

Father, show us from Your Word what You want husbands to do and
be, so that we all are blessed and Christ is glorified. Amen.

2 SCRIPTURE READING

Monday	GENESIS 2:18-24
Tuesday	PROVERBS 18:22; 19:14; ECCLESIASTES 9:9
Wednesday	1 CORINTHIANS 7:1-5; HEBREWS 13:4
Thursday	1 CORINTHIANS 11:3; TITUS 2:2, 6
Friday	COLOSSIANS 3:19; 1 PETER 3:7
Saturday	PHILIPPIANS 2:3-4; 1 TIMOTHY 5:8
Sunday	EPHESIANS 5:28-33

FEATURED SCRIPTURE

*He who loves his wife loves himself. For no one ever hated his own flesh,
but nourishes and cherishes it, just as Christ does the church, because we
are members of his body.* —EPHESIANS 5:28-30

3 ACTIVITY OF THE DAY

Monday

Husbands, do you recognize that you were made to *need* a "helper"? Aside from domestic duties that you two should share, what significant kinds of help can your wife provide? Do you seek such help from her, or do you try to "go it alone"?

_____

_____

_____

Tuesday

Do you thank God for your wife? Do you enjoy life with her today as much as you did when you were engaged? Why or why not?

_____

_____

_____

Wednesday

How committed are both of you to avoiding sexual relations outside of marriage? What part of the Bible's instructions on this topic, if any, troubles you or seems difficult to follow? Talk it over with each other and with the Lord.

_____

_____

_____

Thursday

Husbands, describe what sort of authority you should exercise over your wife. What kind of leadership does she need from you? How is your role affected by the fact that you, in turn, report to Christ as your head? Are you "sound in faith, in love, and in steadfastness"? Be honest.

_____

_____

_____

_____

Friday

Ask your wife in humility, "How can I do a better job of showing you honor? In what ways have I failed to be understanding?" Finally, seek her forgiveness for the times when you were harsh, and tell her you need her to pray that you will grow in patience.

_____

_____

_____

_____

Saturday

When you begin a new day, are you as tuned in to (even excited about) what your wife is facing that day as you are your own interests and responsibilities? If not, how can you change that?

_____

_____

_____

_____

Sunday

Memorize this week's featured Bible passage or your favorite portion from one of the other readings.

4 CONCLUSION

Adam needed a helper, and so do we. In marriage, a husband becomes one flesh with his wife, and together they live for God. We husbands are to reflect Christ both in our leadership and in our service, ready and willing to lay down our lives for our spouses and children. If we truly cherish our wives, we will find it natural to count them as more significant than ourselves.

5 CLOSING PRAYER

Talk to God alone or together about your family, friends, church, and community, as well as about what He is saying to you today through His Word. Then conclude with this:

Make us good husbands and wives, so that
our marriage is pleasing to You and a source
of joy in every season of life. Amen.

Good Wives

*How to be the woman
God intended*

1 OPENING PRAYER

Lord, help me to hear You today, so that I might please You *first* in
my role as a wife to my husband. Show us Your perfect design for
marriage, and enable us to live accordingly. Amen.

2 SCRIPTURE READING

Monday	GENESIS 2:18-24
Tuesday	PROVERBS 12:4; 31:10-24
Wednesday	PROVERBS 31:25-29
Thursday	1 CORINTHIANS 11:3; EPHESIANS 5:22-24, 33; COLOSSIANS 3:18
Friday	PHILIPPIANS 2:3-4
Saturday	PROVERBS 31:30-31; 1 PETER 3:3-6
Sunday	TITUS 2:3-5

FEATURED SCRIPTURE

*Charm is deceitful, and beauty is vain, but a woman who fears the Lord
is to be praised. Give her of the fruit of her hands, and let her works
praise her in the gates.* —PROVERBS 31:30-31

3 ACTIVITY OF THE DAY

Monday

Wives, to what extent is your life about being a helper to your husband? Are you "there" for him in his work and other responsibilities, or does he feel somewhat alone?

_____

_____

_____

Tuesday

Does today's Scripture passage describe you? In what ways? Do you think your husband considers you to be an "excellent wife"? Do your friends see you that way? Explain.

_____

_____

_____

Wednesday

Are you "a woman who fears the Lord"? How would you rate yourself on the other characteristics mentioned in today's reading, such as strength, wisdom, and kindness? Do your husband and children praise you for these traits? Why or why not?

_____

_____

_____

Thursday

What does the Bible mean by asking wives to "submit" to their husbands? Does this command anger you, confuse you, or remind you of the sort of wife you want to be? Why is this idea so controversial today? Do you genuinely respect your husband, as it says in Ephesians 5:33?

_____

_____

_____

_____

Friday

Wives, answer the same questions that husbands were asked last week: When you begin a new day, are you as tuned in to (even excited about) what your husband is facing that day as you are your own interests and responsibilities? If not, how can you change that?

_____

_____

_____

_____

_____

Saturday

Where is the balance between trying to maintain an outward beauty that pleases your husband and the inner, "imperishable beauty of a gentle and quiet spirit"? Which really matters the most to you, and why?

_____

_____

_____

_____

Sunday

Memorize this week's featured Bible passage or your favorite portion from one of the other readings.

4 CONCLUSION

The traits that the Bible ascribes to an excellent wife are numerous: helpful, hardworking, kind, wise, blessed, strong, reverent, faithful, submissive, respectful, unselfish, self-controlled, fearless, inwardly beautiful. Some of what Scripture teaches about wives is offensive to modern ears, but that's all the more reason to listen to what God has said. One thing is clear: Husbands cannot be good husbands without the help of their wives, and wives cannot be good wives without the help of their husbands. We succeed or fail together.

5 CLOSING PRAYER

Talk to God alone or together about your family, friends, church, and community, as well as about what He is saying to you today through His Word. Then conclude with this:

Lord, make me the crown of my husband by being a fit helper with a gentle and quiet spirit. In Jesus's name. Amen.

Good Kids

Jesus loves the little children. . . . All are precious in His sight.

1 OPENING PRAYER

Lord, reveal to us what You would like our children to know at this early stage of their lives. Show us how we can best train and instruct them in Your ways. Amen.

2 SCRIPTURE READING

Monday	1 CORINTHIANS 13:11
Tuesday	EXODUS 20:12
Wednesday	PSALM 139:13-16
Thursday	PSALM 71:17
Friday	PROVERBS 1:8-9; 4:1-9; 22:6; 29:17; EPHESIANS 6:1-4
Saturday	MARK 10:13-16
Sunday	DEUTERONOMY 6:6-9

See also DEUTERONOMY 4:9-10; PSALM 127:3-5; COLOSSIANS 3:20-21; 1 THESSALONIANS 2:11-12

FEATURED SCRIPTURE

"Let the children come to me; do not hinder them, for to such belongs the kingdom of God." —MARK 10:14

3 ACTIVITY OF THE DAY

Monday

How can you help your children realize their need for guidance as they start out in life? How easy are you making it for them to talk to you and ask for advice? Are you available, or are you always seemingly busy with something else?

_____

_____

_____

_____

Tuesday

What does it mean to honor one's parents? Do your kids honor you? How are you teaching them to do so? Is what they see in you worthy of honor?

_____

_____

_____

_____

_____

Wednesday

How can you give your kids a real sense that God made them, loves them, and will guide them on their path throughout life? When are some of the best opportunities to drive this message home?

_____

_____

_____

Thursday

Ask your children at dinnertime: Do you realize that God himself
wants to be your teacher? How do you listen for God's voice? Tell us
all about a time when He taught you something.

_____

_____

_____

_____

Friday

How are you *encouraging* your kids to obey you rather than making
them discouraged or angry? Brainstorm some effective ways of gaining
their respect and obedience. What more can you do to bring them up
in the "discipline and instruction of the Lord"?

_____

_____

_____

Saturday

How well have you impressed upon your children the fact that Jesus
loves them? That they are special in His eyes, not less important than
the grown-ups? How are they responding to Him personally?

Sunday

Memorize this week's featured Bible passage or your favorite portion from one of the other readings.

4 CONCLUSION

God has given parents a great responsibility in raising His children. Primarily through Mom and Dad, He teaches young people the way to eternal life. So obedience to parents is a key biblical mandate. But Jesus also wants children to come to Him, to begin relating to Him directly and walking through their early years with Him. We should do everything we can to introduce children to Jesus.

5 CLOSING PRAYER

Talk to God alone or together about your family, friends, church, and community, as well as about what He is saying to you today through His Word. Then conclude with this:

Lord, help us bring our children to You, and touch them with Your love. Watch over them and mold them into disciples who serve and love You for eternity. Amen.

Acceptance in the Home

None of us is okay, but that's okay.

1 OPENING PRAYER

Father, You not only bear with us despite our sins, but You welcome us into communion with You! Show us how to do the same for one another. In Jesus's name. Amen.

2 SCRIPTURE READING

Monday	MATTHEW 17:17; ACTS 13:17-18
Tuesday	ROMANS 15:1; EPHESIANS 4:1-3
Wednesday	ROMANS 5:8
Thursday	MATTHEW 7:1-5; ROMANS 14:1-4; JAMES 5:9
Friday	MARK 9:37; ROMANS 15:7
Saturday	1 CORINTHIANS 13:7
Sunday	COLOSSIANS 3:12-14

FEATURED SCRIPTURE

Put on then, as God's chosen ones, holy and beloved, compassionate hearts, kindness, humility, meekness, and patience, bearing with one another and, if one has a complaint against another, forgiving each other.

—COLOSSIANS 3:12-13

3 ACTIVITY OF THE DAY

Monday

List some things that you do, or your family does, to displease or dishonor God—things He puts up with rather than punishing you for. Why does He bear with you in spite of these things?

_____

_____

_____

_____

Tuesday

What are some things that your family members routinely do or say that bother you? How can you bear with someone while also asking him or her to stop the offending behavior?

_____

_____

_____

_____

Wednesday

What is the supreme example of God accepting us despite who we are? Explain how this should affect our own behavior.

_____

_____

_____

_____

Thursday

What does it mean to judge someone? From today's Bible passages, what are all the reasons we are in no position to judge someone else? Is any judging going on in your family? If so, why?

_____

_____

_____

_____

Friday

What is the main reason for wholeheartedly accepting other members of your family, despite your different outlooks or ways of doing things? How are your children learning to accept one another's differences?

_____

_____

_____

_____

Saturday

As a family, talk about how willing you all should be to "endure all things" from one another. Tell each other what things are hardest for you to bear with, put up with, or overlook.

Sunday

Memorize this week's featured Bible passage or your favorite portion from one of the other readings.

4 CONCLUSION

Isn't our God practical and realistic? He knows that sometimes the best we sinners can do, especially in the close quarters of a home, is to put up with or endure one another! He sets the example by always bearing with us, so we must strive to be like Him and practice acceptance in the family, rather than crying foul every time we are offended or wronged.

5 CLOSING PRAYER

Talk to God alone or together about your family, friends, church, and community, as well as about what He is saying to you today through His Word. Then conclude with this:

> *Lord, thank You for putting up with us today, even though*
> *we continue to fail You with our disobedience. Teach us to*
> *bear with one another and to rejoice in the unique person You*
> *designed each one of us to be. For Your glory. Amen.*

We Belong to One Another

In the Christian family, we've got each other's backs no matter the cost.

1 OPENING PRAYER

Lord, You have called us to be devoted to one another. Show us what that looks like in our home, and help us move in that direction. Amen.

2 SCRIPTURE READING

Monday	JOSHUA 7 (all)
Tuesday	1 SAMUEL 19:1-5
Wednesday	JOHN 15:12-13
Thursday	ROMANS 12:5, 10; 1 CORINTHIANS 12:15-16
Friday	ACTS 2:42; 1 CORINTHIANS 16:15
Saturday	EPHESIANS 6:16-18
Sunday	PHILIPPIANS 4:14-19

See also 2 TIMOTHY 4:10; TITUS 3:14; HEBREWS 3:12-14

FEATURED SCRIPTURE

"Greater love has no one than this, that someone lay down his life for his friends." —JOHN 15:13

3 ACTIVITY OF THE DAY

Monday

Today's reading is hard to accept, but this much we know: One person's actions can seriously impact the whole group (or family). How might you get your family to understand that you all succeed or fail together?

_____

_____

_____

_____

Tuesday

As Jonathan did for David, we're called to stand by and defend the people we love. Does that describe your family? Explain.

_____

_____

_____

Wednesday

Is every member of your family ready to lay down his or her life for another family member? Really? What might this involve? Discuss this honestly around the dinner table.

_____

_____

_____

_____

Thursday

In a world where we are accustomed to thinking of ourselves mostly as individuals, how can we grasp the fact that our family is a unified whole? Is there any competition in your home that tends to threaten this sense of unity?

_____

_____

_____

_____

Friday

How should being devoted to the family and to one another affect each member's use of time? Workload around the house? Personal belongings? Have your family discuss and agree on some basic rules.

_____

_____

_____

_____

Saturday

Do you think of spiritual battle as something you engage in by yourself, or do you picture your family members fighting side by side?

How can the whole family help a member who's in the heat of some battle at school or work?

_____

_____

_____

_____

Sunday

Memorize this week's featured Bible passage or your favorite portion from one of the other readings.

4 CONCLUSION

It's the Lord's desire that we be devoted, first of all, to the fellowship and service of the saints living under our own roof. Not everything we do for God is centered in the home, but no other calling should draw us away from giving our due to family members. Belonging to one another may result in generous sharing of time, effort, and resources.

5 CLOSING PRAYER

Talk to God alone or together about your family, friends, church, and community, as well as about what He is saying to you today through His Word. Then conclude with this:

Father, never let us desert the members of our own family because we fell in love with our own pursuits. Make us loyal to those You have placed in our lives. For Your glory. Amen.

Time to Fess Up

*If we say we have
no sin, we deceive
ourselves.*

1 OPENING PRAYER

Father, show us how to respond when we fail to live by Your indwelling Spirit and do or say something that offends You. Make us ready to be honest with You and others about our sins. In Jesus's name. Amen.

2 SCRIPTURE READING

Monday	ROMANS 3:9-23; 7:14-25
Tuesday	EZRA 10:1-5; NEHEMIAH 9:1-3
Wednesday	PSALM 32:5; 51:15-17; PROVERBS 28:13
Thursday	PSALM 51:1-12 (see 2 SAMUEL 12:7-10 for context)
Friday	LUKE 15:11-24
Saturday	JAMES 5:16
Sunday	1 JOHN 1:8-9

See also ACTS 19:18-20

FEATURED SCRIPTURE

Confess your sins to one another and pray for one another, that you may be healed. —JAMES 5:16

3 ACTIVITY OF THE DAY

Monday

Discuss with your family the fact that even as Christians, we still wrestle with the power of sin for the time being; we are broken people who constantly do and think and say things that we need to confess. Are we ready to base our expectations for one another on the reality that all family members are battling to control their fallen nature?

_____

_____

_____

_____

Tuesday

Are there any sins that you should confess as a couple rather than as individuals? Also, when should we repent of sinful ways on behalf of the whole body of Christ in our nation or in the world?

_____

_____

_____

_____

Wednesday

Is the confession of sin an important part of your personal prayers? Why or why not? Does the fact that we have been saved by God's grace cause you to ignore the need for daily repentance? Explain.

Thursday

When we do something that hurts another person, whether in or outside the family, whom are we sinning against? Who needs to hear our confession?

Friday

How does God feel when we confess our sins to Him?

Saturday

What would make it easier for a family member to admit when he or she has done something wrong? How should the family respond? By praying together? Forming a plan to help the person overcome that sin?

Sunday

Memorize this week's featured Bible passage or your favorite portion from one of the other readings.

4 CONCLUSION

For centuries, the church has recognized that even though God has forgiven us and promised us eternal life, there is still a place for confessing the sins that we continue to commit while in these mortal bodies. Many churches have downplayed the confession of sins, but when confession is practiced in the family, it brings divine healing and harmony.

5 CLOSING PRAYER

Talk to God alone or together about your family, friends, church, and community, as well as about what He is saying to you today through His Word. Then conclude with this:

> *Most merciful God, we confess that we have sinned against you in thought, word, and deed, by what we have done, and by what we have left undone. We have not loved you with our whole heart; we have not loved our neighbors as ourselves. We are truly sorry and we humbly repent. For the sake of your Son Jesus Christ, have mercy on us and forgive us; that we may delight in your will, and walk in your ways, to the glory of your Name. Amen. —From* The Book of Common Prayer

Forgive One Another

If we want it for ourselves, we have to give it.

1 OPENING PRAYER

Father, we have undeservedly received Your lavish forgiveness and been received into Your eternal family. Now show us how to follow Your example in forgiving those dearest to us. In Jesus's name. Amen.

2 SCRIPTURE READING

Monday	MATTHEW 6:11-15; MARK 11:25
Tuesday	MATTHEW 18:21-22
Wednesday	EXODUS 10:14-20
Thursday	GENESIS 50:15-21
Friday	LUKE 23:34
Saturday	COLOSSIANS 3:12-14
Sunday	EPHESIANS 4:31-32

See also MATTHEW 18:23-35; 2 CORINTHIANS 2:5-7; JAMES 5:16

FEATURED SCRIPTURE

Be kind to one another, tenderhearted, forgiving one another, as God in Christ forgave you. —EPHESIANS 4:32

3 ACTIVITY OF THE DAY

Monday

What happens when we refuse to forgive one another and instead nurse a grudge?

_____

_____

_____

_____

Tuesday

We must forgive over and over and over. What happens in the family when we stop forgiving, or we bring up old offenses?

_____

_____

_____

_____

Wednesday

Why must we keep our guard up rather than simply trusting that a forgiven family member will not fail again? If it happens, why should the whole family, not just a parent, come up with a solution together?

_____

_____

_____

Thursday

Have you ever had someone act badly toward you, only to discover that God turned it into something good? Explain.

_____

_____

_____

_____

Friday

How does making allowance for someone's spiritual immaturity make it easier to forgive the person? Should we forgive only when someone has repented and asked for forgiveness? What did Jesus do?

_____

_____

_____

Saturday

How amazed are you at God's forgiveness? Do you really understand why you don't deserve His mercy? How might coming to terms with this reality make you a more forgiving person at home?

_____

_____

_____

_____

Sunday

Memorize this week's featured Bible passage or your favorite portion from one of the other readings.

4 CONCLUSION

The family is no picnic in paradise; it's a halfway house for forgiven sinners. If we wake up to the fact that we're all works in progress, we won't be so upset or indignant every time we are wronged. We all need constant forgiveness for things we do or say that hurt the people we love. A home where forgiveness flows freely brings glory to God, since a forgiving spirit reflects His very nature. As He does toward us, we should forgive often and without waiting to be asked.

5 CLOSING PRAYER

Talk to God alone or together about your family, friends, church, and community, as well as about what He is saying to you today through His Word. Then conclude with this:

> *As we behold your Son, enthroned on the cross,*
> *stir up in us the fire of your love,*
> *that we may be cleansed from all our sins,*
> *and walk with you in newness of life*
> *singing the praise of him who died*
> *for us and for our salvation. Amen.*
> —*From* Common Worship: Daily Prayer

Humility at Home

The family needs a leader, but what kind of leader?

1 OPENING PRAYER

Jesus, illuminate for us Your servant nature, then help us understand why we must follow in Your footsteps. Amen.

2 SCRIPTURE READING

Monday	LUKE 22:24-26; 1 CORINTHIANS 16:15-16
Tuesday	PROVERBS 18:12
Wednesday	1 PETER 5:5-7
Thursday	PHILIPPIANS 2:5-8
Friday	MATTHEW 11:29
Saturday	JAMES 3:13-15
Sunday	MATTHEW 18:1-4

See also MATTHEW 6:1-4; ROMANS 12:16; EPHESIANS 4:1-3; 5:20-24; 6:1; COLOSSIANS 3:12-13; JAMES 4:10; 1 PETER 3:8-9

FEATURED SCRIPTURE

"Take my yoke upon you, and learn from me, for I am gentle and lowly in heart, and you will find rest for your souls." —MATTHEW 11:29

3 ACTIVITY OF THE DAY

Monday

How should the leader of a Christian home differ from that of other families? What makes a truly good family leader? How are you as a servant?

_____

_____

_____

_____

Tuesday

What happens when a husband takes a domineering approach toward his wife and/or children, rather than a humble one? Describe children you know who came from an oppressive home.

_____

_____

_____

Wednesday

Who in the family should practice humility toward the others? How does a desire for control or recognition get in the way? Can your family make sure that everyone gets a turn at planning a family activity (or solving a family problem) his or her way? Discuss among yourselves.

_____

_____

_____

Thursday

How much did Jesus give up for us? Really think about it. Now, how much are *you* willing to give up in order to become like Jesus? Do you want credit for doing so?

_____

_____

_____

_____

Friday

Was Jesus saying that life is actually easier and more pleasant if we don't try to assert ourselves over others but instead be lowly in heart? Why might this be true?

_____

_____

_____

Saturday

Is there competition among your children? Discuss as a family why we sometimes foolishly think it is important to be better than others rather than let *them* be better in something so they can help us.

_____

_____

_____

_____

Sunday

Memorize this week's featured Bible passage or your favorite portion from one of the other readings.

4 CONCLUSION

Humility, authority, submission . . . the world has its own confused ideas about such things. But God's perspective is completely different. In the Bible we discover that true leaders should be meek and ready to serve, rather than rule like tyrants. The family functions well only when *everyone* practices humility at home.

5 CLOSING PRAYER

Talk to God alone or together about your family, friends, church, and community, as well as about what He is saying to you today through His Word. Then conclude with this:

> *Dear Jesus, You are Master and Lord of the universe,*
> *yet You are also "gentle and lowly in heart." You amaze*
> *and thrill us! Make us into Your likeness, so that by our*
> *humility, Your glory will be evident to all. Amen.*

Upstairs and Downstairs

In God's family, we're all servants meeting one another's needs.

1 OPENING PRAYER

Lord, You came to serve rather than to be served. May we learn to do likewise, starting with our own households. Amen.

2 SCRIPTURE READING

Monday	MARK 10:45; LUKE 4:38-39
Tuesday	LUKE 22:26-27; JOHN 13:3-17
Wednesday	ROMANS 12:13; GALATIANS 6:10
Thursday	2 CORINTHIANS 9:7-12; PHILIPPIANS 4:16-17
Friday	2 CORINTHIANS 4:5; PHILIPPIANS 2:19-21
Saturday	1 TIMOTHY 5:8
Sunday	EPHESIANS 5:1-2

See also GALATIANS 5:13-15; PHILIPPIANS 2:3-8; HEBREWS 1:13-14; 1 PETER 4:10-11

FEATURED SCRIPTURE

"If I then, your Lord and Teacher, have washed your feet, you also ought to wash one another's feet. For I have given you an example, that you also should do just as I have done to you." —JOHN 13:14-15

3 ACTIVITY OF THE DAY

Monday

As Simon's mother-in-law discovered, Jesus came to serve. What is the natural response of anyone whom Jesus has served? How well do each of your family members currently serve the other members?

_____

_____

_____

_____

Tuesday

Why did Jesus wash His disciples' feet at the Last Supper? Why did Simon Peter try to refuse Him? Do you have trouble letting other family members serve you? If so, why?

_____

_____

_____

Wednesday

What is your family doing to meet the basic needs of other Christians in your church, community, and around the world? Talk it over, pray, and make some plans together.

_____

_____

_____

_____

Thursday

What happens when you serve and donate to other Christians in
need? What do they often do in turn? How is God involved? Who
benefits most when someone's needs are met?

_____

_____

_____

_____

Friday

Whose interests do you seek from day to day? Seriously! If you answer
"Jesus," how do people *know* that you are serving Jesus Christ?

_____

_____

_____

_____

Saturday

Examine how each family member's basic needs are being met, not
just for food, clothing, shelter, and transportation, but also for rest,
time alone, social contact, etc. Look for solutions as a family. Then
also discuss what to do about needs among your relatives and family
friends.

_____

_____

_____

_____

Sunday

Memorize this week's featured Bible passage or your favorite portion from one of the other readings.

4 CONCLUSION

According to the apostle Paul, we once were slaves of sin, but now we've been set free to become "slaves of God" (Romans 6:22)! There is great joy and freedom in our slavery—our service to God—and the best way to serve our Lord is to fulfill the needs of His people. In today's world, more and more people are going without their basic needs met, and it's our privilege and calling to do something about it.

5 CLOSING PRAYER

Talk to God alone or together about your family, friends, church, and community, as well as about what He is saying to you today through His Word. Then conclude with this:

> *Lord, as You have served us, help us rise up and serve You*
> *by reaching out to family members and beyond, wherever*
> *there is need. May all that we do result in many people*
> *thanking and blessing You, the Source of all good. Amen.*

The Peaceable Family

We can't afford to act in a merely human way.

1 OPENING PRAYER

O God of Peace, we confess that we do not easily get along with one another. Though You have redeemed us, our "flesh" still leads us into strife with other family members. Teach us a better way. In Jesus's name. Amen.

2 SCRIPTURE READING

Monday	JAMES 3:16-18; 4:1-3
Tuesday	PROVERBS 20:3; 29:22; JAMES 1:19
Wednesday	EPHESIANS 4:26
Thursday	GALATIANS 5:19-20; EPHESIANS 6:4
Friday	EPHESIANS 4:31-32; PHILIPPIANS 4:2-3
Saturday	1 THESSALONIANS 5:23; 2 THESSALONIANS 3:16
Sunday	2 CORINTHIANS 13:11

See also MARK 9:50; 1 CORINTHIANS 3:3; PHILIPPIANS 2:14-15; COLOSSIANS 3:5-8, 15; 1 THESSALONIANS 5:13-14; 2 TIMOTHY 2:23-25; HEBREWS 12:14

FEATURED SCRIPTURE

Finally, brothers, rejoice. Aim for restoration, comfort one another, agree with one another, live in peace; and the God of love and peace will be with you. —2 CORINTHIANS 13:11

3 ACTIVITY OF THE DAY

Monday

Fundamentally, what causes strife in your family? What kind of disorder does it create? And what is the solution?

_____

_____

_____

Tuesday

Do you tend to be a "man [or woman] of wrath"? If so, *why* are you prone to anger? What is the result in your family? How can you become "slow to anger"?

_____

_____

_____

Wednesday

How can you or your spouse be angry without sinning? Why is it important not to let an argument last from one day to the next?

_____

_____

_____

Thursday

How can you minimize the enmity, jealousy, and rivalries that break out between your children? Have you ever provoked your kids to anger? If yes, what might you do differently?

_____

_____

Friday

How can your family intervene *as a group* (not just the parents) when two members are in conflict? Discuss together how Christians can just decide to "put away" all strife. How will you help one another do this?

_____

_____

Saturday

Does your family ask God for help when there's a conflict at home? Why is this important? How do you think a conscious awareness of Jesus's presence in your family could discourage quarreling?

_____

_____

_____

_____

Sunday

Memorize this week's featured Bible passage or your favorite portion from one of the other readings.

4 CONCLUSION

The Bible is full of warnings against fighting with one another. But what Christian family hasn't had more than enough of such conflict? The answer is to look to God for help, invite Him into your home, and then work together as a family, helping one another overcome the tendency toward jealousy and anger.

5 CLOSING PRAYER

Talk to God alone or together about your family, friends, church, and community, as well as about what He is saying to you today through His Word. Then conclude with this:

> *Lord, make us instruments of Your peace. Where there is hatred, let us sow love; where there is injury, pardon; where there is doubt, faith; where there is despair, hope; where there is darkness, light; where there is sadness, joy. O, Divine Master, grant that we may not so much seek to be consoled as to console; to be understood as to understand; to be loved as to love; For it is in giving that we receive; it is in pardoning that we are pardoned; it is in dying that we are born again to eternal life. —Adapted from* "Prayer of Saint Francis"

All for One, and One for All

Unity and harmony are important traits of every Christian home.

1 OPENING PRAYER

O God, You are one, and in Christ You created one faith, one body of followers. Show us how to reflect that unity in our behavior toward one another. Amen.

2 SCRIPTURE READING

Monday	JOHN 10:16; EPHESIANS 2:18-22; COLOSSIANS 1:16-17
Tuesday	EPHESIANS 4:1-3
Wednesday	PSALM 133
Thursday	1 CORINTHIANS 1:10; 2 CORINTHIANS 13:11; PHILIPPIANS 2:1-2
Friday	JOHN 17:20-23
Saturday	EPHESIANS 4:13-16
Sunday	ROMANS 15:5-6

See also ROMANS 12:16; EPHESIANS 4:4; COLOSSIANS 3:14; 1 PETER 3:8-9

May the God of endurance and encouragement grant you to live in such harmony with one another, in accord with Christ Jesus, that together you may with one voice glorify the God and Father of our Lord Jesus Christ.
—ROMANS 15:5-6

3 ACTIVITY OF THE DAY

Monday

Why does God long for His whole family to be one?

_____

_____

_____

Tuesday

What are some things that tend to divide Christians from one another? Discuss as a family what causes divisions at your house. What you are going to do about it?

_____

_____

_____

Wednesday

Recall a time when your family joined together to advance a cause or celebrate one member's achievement. How did that unity feel?

_____

_____

_____

Thursday

Does being "of the same mind" and agreeing together mean we shouldn't have diverse outlooks and opinions? If not, explain how we can differ but still be united.

_____

_____

_____

Friday

What can you do regularly as a family to foster a strong sense of unity not only with one another but with the Lord? What does group worship or prayer offer that you can't get from private devotions?

_____

_____

_____

Saturday

As a family, discuss what's unique and wonderful about each member of your household. How can your differences be a source of unity and harmony?

_____

_____

_____

Sunday

Memorize this week's featured Bible passage or your favorite portion from one of the other readings.

4 CONCLUSION

Though peace in the home is important, a false sort of peace can come from simply ignoring one another and going our separate ways—which is how many families operate in today's frenetic society. But that's not what a Christian family should be like. The aim, rather, is to blend our different instruments—our personalities and callings—into one harmonious symphony that brings honor to God. This won't just happen; we have to work at it.

5 CLOSING PRAYER

Talk to God alone or together about your family, friends, church, and community, as well as about what He is saying to you today through His Word. Then conclude with this:

> *Father, join us to one another and to Your Son, the*
> *Cornerstone, so that our family can be part of a holy*
> *temple in which You are pleased to dwell. Amen.*

The Family That Meets Together

Will it be Facebook or face-to-face?

1 OPENING PRAYER

Lord, just as we are learning to abide in You and to enjoy Your daily company, make us long also to see one another and be mutually encouraged. In Your name. Amen.

2 SCRIPTURE READING

Monday	HEBREWS 10:24-25
Tuesday	1 THESSALONIANS 2:17-20
Wednesday	ROMANS 1:11-12
Thursday	ACTS 2:46-47
Friday	2 JOHN 12; 3 JOHN 13-14
Saturday	2 TIMOTHY 1:3-4
Sunday	1 THESSALONIANS 3:6-10

FEATURED SCRIPTURE

Let us consider how to stir up one another to love and good works, not neglecting to meet together, as is the habit of some, but encouraging one another, and all the more as you see the Day drawing near.

—HEBREWS 10:24-25

3 ACTIVITY OF THE DAY

Monday

Are your family members like the proverbial "ships passing in the night"? If so, why? How effectively can you "stir up one another to love and good works" without actually meeting and talking and praying together as a family?

_____

_____

_____

_____

Tuesday

Ask your family to discuss the idea of a regular family meeting to talk over current events, divide up chores, review family members' needs, pray together, etc. What might they dislike about meeting together? How could these meetings be made fun and appealing?

_____

_____

_____

_____

Wednesday

Does your family usually eat dinner (or some other meal) together? If not, what are you missing out on as a result?

_____

_____

_____

Thursday

Does your family worship *together* when with a larger body of believers on Sunday morning? Or do you go your separate ways while at church? What do you think is best?

_____

_____

_____

Friday

Why did the apostle John, who wrote letters, nevertheless prefer face-to-face contact? Why have Facebook and texting often replaced letters, phone calls, and gatherings today? What are the advantages and drawbacks of these new ways to communicate? What effects, good and bad, are they having on your family?

_____

_____

_____

Saturday

Scan the contents of this devotional guide for a few minutes. Now, in your opinion, how many of the commands given to Christians in the New Testament can be done, and done well, without physically getting together? Explain.

Sunday

Memorize this week's featured Bible passage or your favorite portion from one of the other readings.

4 CONCLUSION

A little over a hundred years ago, family members often lost contact with each other for months or years at a time. Then came modern transport and electronic communication. So today, we have countless ways to stay in contact with loved ones. But somehow we've lost the art of doing so, even when living under the same roof. The Christian family that wants to serve Jesus well cannot do so without meeting together often.

5 CLOSING PRAYER

Talk to God alone or together about your family, friends, church, and community, as well as about what He is saying to you today through His Word. Then conclude with this:

> *Lord, thank You for creating our family. Now teach us once*
> *again how to act like a family, not neglecting to meet*
> *together, as is the habit of some. For Your glory. Amen.*

The Hospitable Home

Knock, knock—who's there? Might it be Jesus?

1 OPENING PRAYER

Father, You have welcomed us into Your kingdom with open arms. So give us wisdom as we try to follow Your example and show hospitality toward others. In Jesus's name. Amen.

2 SCRIPTURE READING

Monday	GENESIS 18:1-8
Tuesday	LUKE 2:6-7; 7:44-47; JOHN 1:9-13; 13:20
Wednesday	ROMANS 12:13; 15:7; 16:1-2; 1 PETER 4:8-9
Thursday	MATTHEW 25:31-46; LUKE 14:12-14
Friday	GENESIS 19:1-3; HEBREWS 13:1-2
Saturday	2 JOHN 9-11; 3 JOHN 9-10
Sunday	3 JOHN 5-8

See also HEBREWS 11:31

FEATURED SCRIPTURE

Welcome one another as Christ has welcomed you, for the glory of God.
—ROMANS 15:7

3 ACTIVITY OF THE DAY

Monday

Hospitality begins with welcoming God into your life and family. How ready are you to recognize and serve Him no matter what method He uses to "knock on your door"?

_____

_____

_____

_____

Tuesday

Why is it common for people to say they believe in God but balk at welcoming Jesus into their lives? How does Jesus feel about being refused hospitality?

_____

_____

_____

_____

Wednesday

Discuss as a family why it is powerful love to invite people—especially other Christians—into your home. What does it do for them? Who in your family is good at making people feel welcome? Whom would you like to invite over?

_____

_____

_____

Thursday

Are there any single-parent families or poor people you know who could benefit by being fed at your house a few times? Does your family know anyone who needs a break from babysitting or watching an elderly person for a day?

_____

_____

_____

_____

Friday

How does your family feel about showing hospitality to strangers, including non-Christians? What excites or frightens you about doing it? What is the danger in *not* opening your home to strangers?

_____

_____

_____

_____

Saturday

When should you purposefully avoid taking someone into your home? What's the difference between unbelievers in general and false teachers who are actively working against the gospel?

_____

_____

_____

_____

Sunday

Memorize this week's featured Bible passage or your favorite portion from one of the other readings.

4 CONCLUSION

It's not uncommon today for even next-door neighbors to remain complete strangers. So a Christian home that opens its doors and practices generous hospitality might become a welcome refuge in such a private, cocooned society. To obey and please our Lord, we should be quick to invite fellow Christians into our homes, as well as anyone else in need.

5 CLOSING PRAYER

Talk to God alone or together about your family, friends, church, and community, as well as about what He is saying to you today through His Word. Then conclude with this:

> *Lord, when You come to our door, whether in the form*
> *of a fellow Christian, a needy soul, or even an angel, help*
> *our family to recognize You and welcome You in. Amen.*

Good Works

We do good not so that we can be saved but because we are saved.

1 OPENING PRAYER

Father, thank You for rescuing us from death. Now show us from Your Word what it means to live in a manner worthy of You. In Jesus's name. Amen.

2 SCRIPTURE READING

Monday	EPHESIANS 2:8-10; TITUS 3:4-8
Tuesday	ROMANS 15:2; 1 CORINTHIANS 10:24
Wednesday	GALATIANS 6:9-10; 2 THESSALONIANS 3:10-13; HEBREWS 10:24
Thursday	2 TIMOTHY 3:16-17
Friday	1 TIMOTHY 5:9-10; TITUS 2:7; 3:14
Saturday	1 THESSALONIANS 5:15; 1 PETER 3:10-11
Sunday	COLOSSIANS 1:9-10

See also HEBREWS 6:10; 13:16; JAMES 3:13; 1 PETER 4:19

FEATURED SCRIPTURE

We are his workmanship, created in Christ Jesus for good works, which God prepared beforehand, that we should walk in them. —EPHESIANS 2:10

3 ACTIVITY OF THE DAY

Monday

Has the fact that we, in the church, are not *saved* by good works caused us to be less concerned about even doing them? What should be the connection between being saved and doing good works?

_____

_____

_____

_____

Tuesday

When a natural disaster or other tragedy occurs, should Christians be the first ones to help out? Why or why not? When are church activities more important than community involvement?

_____

_____

_____

_____

Wednesday

Why is it easy to grow weary in doing good? What are some effective ways of motivating one another in your family to do good in the name of the Lord? How can you stir one another up?

_____

_____

_____

_____

Thursday

How can the Bible equip your family for every good work?

_____

_____

_____

_____

Friday

As a family, help each member reach out to two people beyond the home who would really benefit from his or her practical help and concern.

_____

_____

_____

Saturday

Identify a family—possibly even one that's been unfriendly toward you—in need of your love. Then do them a good deed that costs time, if not money.

_____

_____

_____

_____

Sunday

Memorize this week's featured Bible passage or your favorite portion from one of the other readings.

4 CONCLUSION

Historically, Christians have been at the forefront of efforts to make life better for everyone, not just those in the church. Good works should be on our to-do lists because our Lord gave us this assignment. He does not want us to withdraw from society and leave urgent needs in the community to others while we organize another church social or Bible study. Since God plans to renew the earth, not just individuals, there's work to do even now, and we are His agents.

5 CLOSING PRAYER

Talk to God alone or together about your family, friends, church, and community, as well as about what He is saying to you today through His Word. Then conclude with this:

> *Lord, stir us up to do the good works that You have called us to. Strengthen us to help others even when the effort seems futile or the rewards few. We pray in Your name. Amen.*

The Almighty & the Dollar—1

We can't worship both God and money.

1 OPENING PRAYER

Father, forgive us for acting like the Israelites in the wilderness, who grumbled and fretted about where they would get their next meal. Teach us, instead, to trust You for all our needs. In Jesus's name. Amen.

2 SCRIPTURE READING

Monday	PSALM 84:11; JOHN 3:27; JAMES 1:17
Tuesday	MATTHEW 6:11; 7:7-11; HEBREWS 13:15-16
Wednesday	LUKE 12:22-32
Thursday	MATTHEW 6:19-21, 24; LUKE 12:15; 1 TIMOTHY 6:10, 17-19
Friday	2 CORINTHIANS 8:1-7
Saturday	1 TIMOTHY 6:6-9; HEBREWS 13:5
Sunday	JAMES 5:1-6

FEATURED SCRIPTURE

Keep your life free from love of money, and be content with what you have, for he has said, "I will never leave you nor forsake you." —HEBREWS 13:5

3 ACTIVITY OF THE DAY

Monday

How can you help your family recognize in a fresh way that everything we have, including our very lives, is a gift from God? What are some things we tend to take for granted?

_____

_____

_____

Tuesday

Does your family join together to ask for something you need from God, and to thank Him for what He has given? Explain. Why is this better than just going to God individually? Why does He even want us to ask?

_____

_____

_____

_____

Wednesday

What happens in your family when finances grow tight? When a parent loses his or her job? Is your response different from that of a non-Christian family? Why or why not?

_____

_____

_____

_____

Thursday

Do you and your family treasure the Lord far above anything else? Why or why not? Discuss as a family what problems have been caused in your home by the love of money or possessions.

_____

_____

_____

Friday

The solution to all our struggles with money is to do as the churches of Macedonia did, which was to "[give] themselves first to the Lord." What does that mean, and what was the result for those Christians?

_____

_____

_____

_____

Saturday

Why is contentment so rare in today's world? What are the benefits of contentment? What should enable us to be content? How content is your family with what they have?

_____

_____

_____

_____

Sunday

Memorize this week's featured Bible passage or your favorite portion from one of the other readings.

4 CONCLUSION

It's very hard for Christians living in a materialistic, consumer-oriented society not to follow suit and become materialists themselves. We lose the ability to distinguish between needs and wants, then we find ourselves spending much of our resources to make life more enjoyable and comfortable. We should ask how the Lord sees us: Are we guilty of trying to love both God and money?

5 CLOSING PRAYER

Talk to God alone or together about your family, friends, church, and community, as well as about what He is saying to you today through His Word. Then conclude with this:

Lord, thank You for every good and perfect gift. Satisfy us above all with Your love, so that we are content in all things and free to worship You, and You alone, forever. In Jesus's name. Amen.

The Almighty & the Dollar—2

When we're free from the love of money, we're able to share.

1 OPENING PRAYER

Lord, convict us when we fail to share Your abundant gifts with those You bring to our attention. And teach us what You have said about our becoming good stewards, so that many will turn to You in thanks. Amen.

2 SCRIPTURE READING

Monday	PROVERBS 14:21, 31; 19:17; ISAIAH 58:6-8
Tuesday	ACTS 2:44-45; ROMANS 15:25-27
Wednesday	2 CORINTHIANS 8:13-15
Thursday	MATTHEW 5:42; ROMANS 12:20-21
Friday	JAMES 2:14-17; 1 JOHN 3:17-18
Saturday	1 CORINTHIANS 13:3; 2 CORINTHIANS 9:6-8
Sunday	LUKE 6:30-31

See also LUKE 3:10-11; 6:30-31; GALATIANS 2:10

And all who believed were together and had all things in common. And they were selling their possessions and belongings and distributing the proceeds to all, as any had need. —ACTS 2:44-45

3 ACTIVITY OF THE DAY

Monday

Our God is passionate about the poor. When you see starving children on TV, are you outraged and heartbroken too? What is your family doing about it?

_____

_____

_____

_____

Tuesday

How does coming to know God's love for us set us free to share resources generously with other believers? What can you do to encourage more sharing (whether of money or the use of possessions) within your family, and with others in the faith?

_____

_____

_____

_____

Wednesday

Has your family ever needed financial help from others? If not, can you imagine a circumstance when that might happen? What can you do to prepare for such a day?

_____

_____

_____

Thursday

How do you know when a person's or organization's appeal for contributions is something the Lord wants you to respond to? What happens when you give to others in need despite their indifference or hostility toward you?

_____

_____

_____

_____

Friday

Describe the connection between your faith in Christ and your use of money or possessions. How do we know our faith is the real thing?

_____

_____

_____

Saturday

When we share with others, does it matter to God what our motivation and attitude are, as long as we give? Explain.

_____

_____

_____

Sunday

Memorize this week's featured Bible passage or your favorite portion from one of the other readings.

4 CONCLUSION

As a result of modern media, we witness every day the suffering of impoverished Christians and others around the world. With this awareness comes great responsibility. In joy, we are called to share our resources with those near and far. We must let our Lord guide our families in every financial decision. Then when we finally see Him, He will be able to say, "Well done, good and faithful servants."

5 CLOSING PRAYER

Talk to God alone or together about your family, friends, church, and community, as well as about what He is saying to you today through His Word. Then conclude with this:

> *Father, everything we have is Yours. Make us cheerful givers to anyone in need, and open our eyes to see that in giving to others, we are giving back to You. In Jesus's name. Amen.*

Worship While You Work

The world lives for the weekends, but should we?

1 OPENING PRAYER

Lord, the need to work for a living is an unpleasant reality for many of us. Help us to reevaluate work from Your perspective instead of adopting our culture's attitude. Thank You for all Your work on our behalf. Amen.

2 SCRIPTURE READING

Monday	GENESIS 1:27-28; GENESIS 2:2-3
Tuesday	GENESIS 3:17-19; ECCLESIASTES 5:18-19
Wednesday	MARK 6:3; ACTS 18:1-3
Thursday	ROMANS 14:7-8; 1 CORINTHIANS 4:1-2; COLOSSIANS 3:17, 23-24
Friday	EPHESIANS 6:5-8
Saturday	EPHESIANS 4:28; 1 THESSALONIANS 4:10-12
Sunday	1 CORINTHIANS 15:58

See also NEHEMIAH 4:7-23; PSALM 104:23; 1 CORINTHIANS 3:10-15

Whatever you do, work heartily, as for the Lord and not for men, knowing that from the Lord you will receive the inheritance as your reward. You are serving the Lord Christ. —COLOSSIANS 3:23-24

3 ACTIVITY OF THE DAY

Monday

Why is work basically a good thing that makes life meaningful? Do your family members see it that way? Why or why not? Also discuss with them why we take time to rest.

_____

_____

_____

_____

Tuesday

Describe the negative parts of your job that likely stem from the fall of mankind in the Garden of Eden. How can you find enjoyment in your job anyway?

_____

_____

_____

_____

Wednesday

How is your perspective on work influenced by the realization that both Jesus and Paul performed manual labor?

_____

_____

_____

_____

Thursday

As a family, discuss the fact that our lives are not our own, but rather we are servants of Jesus Christ. How does it help you to know that your real employer is the Lord himself? Ask your kids if they do their homework and chores "as for the Lord."

_____

_____

_____

_____

Friday

What should be our attitude as we dig into our work each day? How does God feel about it?

_____

_____

_____

_____

Saturday

Besides earning a living for ourselves and our family, what are some other reasons for performing steady work? How can you help unemployed family or church members find a job?

_____

_____

Sunday

Memorize this week's featured Bible passage or your favorite portion from one of the other readings.

4 CONCLUSION

The Lord has been honest with us about work. It's both wonderful and terrible, for reasons that the book of Genesis makes clear. So what are we to do? The answer is that we work heartily "as for the Lord." When we do that, even the worst drudgery or overbearing boss can often become tolerable. And we look forward to our eternal life in the new earth, when work—even hard work—will be nothing but pure bliss.

5 CLOSING PRAYER

Talk to God alone or together about your family, friends, church, and community, as well as about what He is saying to you today through His Word. Then conclude with this:

Father, as long as we live, we live for You. And by working,
we reflect Your image. Help us, then, to do work that
honors You and helps others. In Jesus's name. Amen.

To Boldly Go . . .

Mustering up the courage to do what you're called to do requires help from family members.

1 OPENING PRAYER

Father, show us this week what You want us to know about courage, then actually *grant* us the courage to act on Your commands. In Jesus's name. Amen.

2 SCRIPTURE READING

Monday	Numbers 13:17-20; John 12:42-43; Hebrews 11:32-38
Tuesday	Psalm 27:14; 31:24; Isaiah 40:31; Acts 23:10-11
Wednesday	1 Samuel 17:22-24, 32-37, 41-47
Thursday	Philippians 1:14; Hebrews 12:3-4
Friday	Acts 28:13-16; Romans 1:11-12; Hebrews 10:24-25
Saturday	1 Thessalonians 2:12; 5:9-11, 14
Sunday	Deuteronomy 3:26-28; 1 Thessalonians 4:16-18

FEATURED SCRIPTURE

For God has not destined us for wrath, but to obtain salvation through our Lord Jesus Christ, who died for us so that whether we are awake or asleep we might live with him. Therefore encourage one another and build one another up, just as you are doing. —I THESSALONIANS 5:9-11

3 ACTIVITY OF THE DAY

Monday

Discuss with family members whether you find it easy or hard to be a follower of Jesus. When does it take courage to obey Him, and what might happen if you did? What sort of courage would it take to be a Christian in Syria or Egypt or North Korea?

_____

_____

_____

Tuesday

How helpful is it to seek encouragement directly from the Lord? Describe how you try to listen to His voice and wait for His response.

_____

_____

Wednesday

As a family, try to think of instances when an attack on the Lord's reputation made you angry. How did your desire to see Him glorified give you courage to act on behalf of Him or His people?

Thursday

Sometimes we find courage ourselves by looking at what others have done. Whose example has emboldened you? Who looks to *you* as an example?

Friday

What does it do for you simply to have other family members or friends present with you when you most need some extra courage?

Saturday

God commands us to encourage one another. At dinner, ask each family member to identify an assignment from the Lord that he or she is putting off out of fear. Then have everyone say things to help the member feel more courageous and get started.

_____

_____

Sunday

How prepared are you to recite God's own words when encouraging someone? Reflect on whether more Bible study or memorization might equip you to become a better encourager.

_____

_____

4 CONCLUSION

In countries like the United States, where freedom and prosperity have been the rule, Christians haven't needed much courage to follow Christ. But in many other nations, being loyal to Jesus is a sacrifice that requires great bravery. No matter what our circumstances are, we cannot stay true to the Lord without the courage we obtain from Him and our fellow believers. Family members, encourage one another!

5 CLOSING PRAYER

Talk to God alone or together about your family, friends, church, and community, as well as about what He is saying to you today through His Word. Then conclude with this:

> *Lord, for Your example, and for Your courageous*
> *followers all around the world, we thank You. Never let*
> *us shrink back from obeying You, but instead remind us*
> *that "the battle is the Lord's." For Your glory. Amen.*

A House of Honor

In a Christian family, everyone should feel special.

1 OPENING PRAYER

Lord, You've given us a lot of instructions about honoring others in our family and beyond. Help us to grasp the importance of this command, and grant us the power to obey You. In Your name. Amen.

2 SCRIPTURE READING

Monday	PROVERBS 10:18; EPHESIANS 4:29-31; 5:4; JAMES 4:11-12
Tuesday	LUKE 14:8-11
Wednesday	JOHN 12:26
Thursday	ROMANS 12:10; PHILIPPIANS 2:3; 1 THESSALONIANS 2:19-20; 1 PETER 2:17
Friday	ROMANS 16:1-2; 1 CORINTHIANS 16:17-18; PHILIPPIANS 2:25-30
Saturday	1 CORINTHIANS 1:27-29; 12:21-26; JAMES 2:1-9
Sunday	PHILIPPIANS 4:8

See also EPHESIANS 6:1-3; 1 PETER 3:7

Love one another with brotherly affection. Outdo one another in showing honor. —ROMANS 12:10

3 ACTIVITY OF THE DAY

Monday

Is any slander going on at your house, whether against a family member or someone else not present? If so, why? How can you and your whole family teach a person to stop dishonoring others?

_____

_____

_____

Tuesday

Are you guilty of always craving honor from other people? If so, why? Who in your family seems intent on gaining recognition? Is it a healthy kind of need or a problem that ought to be addressed?

_____

_____

_____

Wednesday

What must you do to honor and receive honor from God? You know that He already loves you, but are you anxious to please Him every day by your thoughts, words, and actions? Reflect on this.

_____

_____

_____

Thursday

How quick are you to applaud another family member when he or
she does something well? Brainstorm as a family some ways to honor
one another often. What kind of celebrations would you all like to
adopt as a family tradition?

_____

_____

_____

Friday

Name some other believers whom your family would like to commend for their service to Christ. Beyond just words, how can you
make such people feel honored?

_____

_____

_____

Saturday

Be honest—do you tend to honor the bright, the beautiful, the cel-
ebrated, the successful? Why? How can you and your whole family

practice honoring the lowly and "less honorable," whether in your family, church, or community?

_____

_____

_____

_____

Sunday

Memorize this week's featured Bible passage or your favorite portion from one of the other readings.

4 CONCLUSION

There's no room in the Christian home for slander or corrupting talk of any kind. Instead, we are commanded to *outdo* one another in showing honor! We should never strive to puff ourselves up, but rather let our Lord honor us for serving Him faithfully. Lastly, we should make a special effort to honor and commend those who are often forgotten and most in need of our high five or pat on the back.

5 CLOSING PRAYER

Talk to God alone or together about your family, friends, church, and community, as well as about what He is saying to you today through His Word. Then conclude with this:

Blessing and glory and wisdom and thanksgiving and honor and power and might be to You, our God, forever and ever! Amen.

Sharing the Load

A heavy-duty command for Christian families

1 OPENING PRAYER

You, Lord, have lifted our burdens and set us on the road to eternal life. Likewise, show us how to lighten the loads of our fellow travelers. Amen.

2 SCRIPTURE READING

Monday	PSALM 38:4; ROMANS 7:18-24
Tuesday	EXODUS 6:5-7; MATTHEW 11:28; 1 PETER 2:24-25
Wednesday	ECCLESIASTES 4:9
Thursday	ROMANS 14:13–15:1
Friday	MARK 7:8; LUKE 11:46; COLOSSIANS 2:20-23
Saturday	GALATIANS 6:2
Sunday	HEBREWS 12:1-2

See also MARK 15:21; 1 THESSALONIANS 5:14

FEATURED SCRIPTURE

Bear one another's burdens, and so fulfill the law of Christ.

—GALATIANS 6:2

3 ACTIVITY OF THE DAY

Monday

How does it feel to be a person who keeps violating what you know to be right? To what degree has becoming a Christian relieved you of this burden? Are you looking forward to someday being a sinless, perfect creature? What do you think that will be like?

_____

_____

_____

Tuesday

How did our Lord take the weight of our sins upon himself? Is this truth just something you believe intellectually, or do you feel genuinely relieved and thankful for what He did to remove your load? Why?

_____

_____

_____

Wednesday

Is it enough just to feel God's forgiveness, or do we sometimes also need to have friends or family members lighten our load by forgiving us and helping us deal with the consequences of our actions? Explain.

_____

_____

_____

Thursday

How should we respond when another Christian feels obligated to follow some rule or practice that we don't believe necessary according to Scripture?

_____

_____

_____

_____

Friday

Is everything we consider a sin really a sin, or is it just a rule we learned somewhere? How can we avoid laying unnecessary burdens on our children?

_____

_____

_____

_____

Saturday

What other kinds of burdens should we bear for one another? Discuss as a family the importance of helping someone else right a wrong. Ask, How do each of you feel when you have to help clean up a mess that another family member made?

_____

_____

_____

_____

Sunday

Memorize this week's featured Bible passage or your favorite portion from one of the other readings.

4 CONCLUSION

We're used to the idea that when Mom needs help carrying in the groceries, everybody grabs a sack or two. What happens, though, if someone's burden is not milk and eggs but sin and its results? Few things in the Christian family are an individual matter. When good things happen, we all rejoice together; when wrongs are done that weigh heavily, we all step forward to help bear the consequences.

5 CLOSING PRAYER

Talk to God alone or together about your family, friends, church, and community, as well as about what He is saying to you today through His Word. Then conclude with this:

Father, help us to lay aside every weight or sin that clings
so closely. And as we do so, lead us to lift the weight
off of others' shoulders. For Your sake. Amen.

Your Pain Is My Pain

When one part of the body hurts, every part feels it.

1 OPENING PRAYER

Father, You know all about pain, since Your own Son underwent great suffering on our behalf. Teach us how to weep with those who weep. In Jesus's name. Amen.

2 SCRIPTURE READING

Monday	GENESIS 3:16-19; PSALM 119:67
Tuesday	ROMANS 5:3-5; PHILIPPIANS 3:8-11
Wednesday	ROMANS 8:16-19; 2 CORINTHIANS 11:23-29
Thursday	PROVERBS 25:20; JOHN 11:33; ROMANS 12:15; HEBREWS 13:3
Friday	1 CORINTHIANS 12:26
Saturday	2 CORINTHIANS 4:16-18; REVELATION 21:4
Sunday	2 TIMOTHY 2:3-7

FEATURED SCRIPTURE

If one member suffers, all suffer together; if one member is honored, all rejoice together. —1 CORINTHIANS 12:26

3 ACTIVITY OF THE DAY

Monday

What are some instances in which you suffered pain as the result of disobeying God? Humbly share these stories with your family.

_____

_____

_____

_____

Tuesday

How and why does suffering often lead to good? What sort of good?

_____

_____

_____

_____

Wednesday

What does it mean to share in Jesus's sufferings, and why must we do it? Put yourself in the place of believers far away who are living in refugee camps or undergoing persecution. Do you feel their suffering?

_____

_____

_____

_____

Thursday

Why is it important to *empathize* with someone's pain rather than downplay it or try to cheer them up? How do you feel when someone you've confided in doesn't seem to hurt with you?

_____

_____

_____

_____

Friday

In a family meeting, ask if anyone is hurting or disappointed or disillusioned about anything. Then as a family, hurt with that person by telling the family member what compassionate thoughts or feelings you have about his or her pain.

_____

_____

_____

_____

Saturday

How could the apostle Paul describe the immense suffering in this present world as "light momentary affliction"? How does your vision of life in the resurrected earth help you endure pain here and now?

_____

_____

_____

_____

Sunday

Memorize this week's featured Bible passage or your favorite portion from one of the other readings.

4 CONCLUSION

Every one of us experiences deep pain at times. But when all is well and life seems good, we're still not out of the woods. That's because "if one member suffers, all suffer together." If even one fellow Christian in our family, church, or a distant land is hurting, we should be, like Jesus, "deeply moved" and "greatly troubled." No wonder we all look forward to the day when mourning, crying, and pain shall be no more!

5 CLOSING PRAYER

Talk to God alone or together about your family, friends, church, and community, as well as about what He is saying to you today through His Word. Then conclude with this:

> *Lord, help us as a family to rejoice in our sufferings, knowing that suffering produces endurance, and endurance produces character, and character produces hope. Thank You, most of all, for a chance to become more like You. Amen.*

Singular Service

Meditations for single adults and those who love them

1 OPENING PRAYER

O Lord, I am alone, yet not alone, for You are here beside me. Speak to me this week and encourage me to follow the path You have laid out for me. In Jesus's name. Amen.

2 SCRIPTURE READING

Monday	GENESIS 2:18
Tuesday	PSALM 23:4; 25:16-18; 62:1-2
Wednesday	ISAIAH 40:28-31; 54:5; HOSEA 2:19-20
Thursday	MATTHEW 22:30, 35-40
Friday	1 CORINTHIANS 7:32-38
Saturday	2 CORINTHIANS 6:14-15; 1 PETER 5:6-7
Sunday	PHILIPPIANS 4:11-13

FEATURED SCRIPTURE

For your Maker is your husband,
the Lord of hosts is his name;
and the Holy One of Israel is your Redeemer,
the God of the whole earth he is called. —ISAIAH 54:5

3 ACTIVITY OF THE DAY

Monday

Why is it generally not good to be alone? What are the benefits of being single? What more can you do to form satisfying, meaningful friendships, especially with members of the same sex?

_____

_____

_____

_____

Tuesday

How are you using your singleness as an opportunity to deepen your relationship to God?

_____

_____

_____

_____

Wednesday

What are some of God's promises that might be especially important for single people?

_____

_____

_____

Thursday

Since there will be no marriage in heaven, you have an advantage over people who fall into depending too much on their spouse. How successful are you at loving the Lord more than anything or anyone else?

_____

_____

_____

_____

Friday

Since a single person is more able to concentrate on "the things of the Lord," survey the contents of this book and ask yourself: Which commands are easier for singles to act upon than Christians who are married?

_____

_____

_____

_____

Saturday

Have you been tempted to escape your single status by marrying an unbeliever? Why or why not? How can you cast on God all your anxieties about the future?

_____

_____

_____

_____

Sunday

Memorize this week's featured Bible passage or your favorite portion from one of the other readings.

4 CONCLUSION

Nearly all of the biblical commands for Christians apply to single adults as much as they do to married people. But since there's no spouse and often no children to relate to at home, singles should grab this opportunity to work with the Lord in making their friendships especially pleasing to Him. In any case, it's not good for a person to be alone (Genesis 2:18). So if you're single, or you care deeply about someone who is, do everything you can to make sure no one is lonely or left out of the rich relationships available to us all in Christ.

5 CLOSING PRAYER

Talk to God about your family, friends, church, and community, as well as about what He is saying to you today through His Word. Then conclude with this:

> *Father, teach us in every circumstance to be*
> *content, knowing that we can do all things*
> *through Your strength. In Jesus's name. Amen.*

Warm Comforters

*Better, even, than a cup of
coffee and a good book*

1 OPENING PRAYER

Lord, You know from Your own experience on earth that this is a troubling place. We are constantly upset by many trials. Please teach us how to draw upon Your comfort and to pass it along to others. Amen.

2 SCRIPTURE READING

Monday	PSALM 23:4
Tuesday	PSALM 119:50-52, 76
Wednesday	ISAIAH 40:1-2; 2 CORINTHIANS 2:5-8
Thursday	ACTS 9:31; ROMANS 15:13
Friday	2 CORINTHIANS 1:3-7; 7:5-7; 13:11; PHILEMON 6-7
Saturday	ISAIAH 66:12-13; 2 THESSALONIANS 2:16-17
Sunday	JOHN 14:25-28

FEATURED SCRIPTURE

Blessed be the God and Father of our Lord Jesus Christ, the Father of mercies and God of all comfort, who comforts us in all our affliction, so that we may be able to comfort those who are in any affliction, with the comfort with which we ourselves are comforted by God. —2 CORINTHIANS 1:3-4

3 ACTIVITY OF THE DAY

Monday

How comforting is it to know that the Lord is guiding, disciplining, and protecting you on your journey through life? In what ways can you do the same for your children?

_____

_____

_____

_____

Tuesday

Describe the comfort you obtain from God's promises in Scripture. What can you do to become more familiar with His promises?

_____

_____

_____

_____

Wednesday

How does God feel about a person who is suffering as a result of some sin(s)? How can your family bring comfort to a family member who's in the same predicament?

_____

_____

_____

_____

Thursday

Have you ever received comfort directly from the Holy Spirit when
you needed it? Explain. How is this better than the comfort that was
available to God's people prior to Jesus's death?

_____

_____

_____

Friday

Most of the comfort we receive from God comes indirectly through
one another. Discuss as a family what you each find most comforting
when you need it. Just having a person be with you? A hug? A good
meal? What else?

_____

_____

_____

Saturday

Are you comforted knowing that someday all will be well? That
we've been promised *eternal* comfort? Does this promise help you get
through hard times now? Why or why not?

_____

_____

_____

_____

Sunday

Memorize this week's featured Bible passage or your favorite portion from one of the other readings.

4 CONCLUSION

God is the great comforter. This is another of His attributes that He wants us to emulate, so that any comfort He gives to us can also be imparted to those in our family or community who need solace. But in order to console others, we must continue to draw upon God's comfort ourselves. We do this by listening quietly to Him, soaking in His promises, accepting His forgiveness, and trying to obey His every command.

5 CLOSING PRAYER

Talk to God alone or together about your family, friends, church, and community, as well as about what He is saying to you today through His Word. Then conclude with this:

Father, wrap Your arms around us like a warm quilt, and prompt us to invite in anyone who's been left out in the cold, thereby sharing the comfort that only You can give. In Jesus's name. Amen.

Speak No Lies

Tell the truth, the whole truth, and nothing but the truth.

1 OPENING PRAYER

Lord, You are the way, the truth, and the life. Help us to put off our old self with its practices, which include evading the truth and deceiving others whenever we are driven by pride, fear, or shame. Amen.

2 SCRIPTURE READING

Monday	PSALM 14:1-3; JEREMIAH 9:5-6; JOHN 8:42-44; COLOSSIANS 3:9-10
Tuesday	PSALM 5:8-10; MARK 7:20-23
Wednesday	LEVITICUS 19:11-12; PSALM 101:7; PROVERBS 6:16-19; 12:22; ZECHARIAH 8:16-17
Thursday	ACTS 5:3-5; 1 JOHN 4:20
Friday	EPHESIANS 4:15-16, 25
Saturday	PSALM 34:12-14
Sunday	1 PETER 2:22

FEATURED SCRIPTURE

Having put away falsehood, let each one of you speak the truth with his neighbor, for we are members one of another. —EPHESIANS 4:25

3 ACTIVITY OF THE DAY

Monday

Does knowing that even as Christians we're all still prone to falsehood help you detect or anticipate problems in your family? Explain. How can you make your children less susceptible to the lies they may be told by friends, teachers, textbooks, other media?

_____

_____

_____

_____

Tuesday

What did Jesus mean when He said that deceit "defiles" the person who speaks it? Ask family members to describe how they felt when they told a lie. What made them lie? Shame? Fear? Something else?

_____

_____

_____

_____

Wednesday

How strongly does God seem to feel about a lying tongue—in other words, about the practice of deceit? Have your family members taken this to heart? Explain. (Or talk it over with them.)

_____

_____

_____

Thursday

Answer for yourself, or discuss as a couple: Have you ever tried to deceive God? What happened? Also, is there some area of life in which you may be trying to deceive yourself? Explain.

_____

_____

_____

_____

Friday

How crucial is speaking the truth for building unity in your family and in your church? Do you tend to speak the truth without love, or to love without speaking the truth? If so, why? How can you practice *both* truth and love in your relationships?

_____

_____

_____

_____

Saturday

How do you feel when someone is clearly being honest? How do you feel when *you* stop trying to deceive and choose to "come clean"? Is this a key to the "good life"? Why?

_____

_____

_____

Sunday

Memorize this week's featured Bible passage or your favorite portion from one of the other readings.

4 CONCLUSION

Unfortunately, telling lies is the norm in our fallen world, practiced not just by overreaching advertisers or corrupt politicians but by everyone who is controlled by his or her fallen nature. On the other hand, telling the truth should be a hallmark of the new nature that God has given us. So we must strive mightily, with God's help, to speak the truth at home, at church, and in society. We must also be honest with God, who cannot be deceived anyway, and with ourselves, so that we see ourselves as God does.

5 CLOSING PRAYER

Talk to God alone or together about your family, friends, church, and community, as well as about what He is saying to you today through His Word. Then conclude with this:

> *Father, we want to be people who reflect Your own*
> *nature. So keep our tongues from evil and our lips*
> *from speaking deceit. Help us to turn away from*
> *evil and do good. For Your glory. Amen.*

A Family Set Apart

"You shall be holy, for I the Lord your God am holy."

1 OPENING PRAYER

Lord, thank You for choosing us before the foundation of the world to be Your own. Make us into a holy and blameless people who by our character bring glory to Your name. Amen.

2 SCRIPTURE READING

Monday	LEVITICUS 19:1-2; JOHN 17:6-13; EPHESIANS 1:4
Tuesday	JOHN 15:19; 17:14-19
Wednesday	ROMANS 12:1-2; 2 TIMOTHY 2:20-21; 1 PETER 2:4-9
Thursday	2 CORINTHIANS 6:14-17; 2 TIMOTHY 3:2-5
Friday	PHILIPPIANS 3:19-21; HEBREWS 11:13-16; 1 PETER 2:10-11
Saturday	COLOSSIANS 1:21-23; HEBREWS 12:14; 1 PETER 1:14-17; 2 PETER 3:11-14
Sunday	EPHESIANS 2:19-22

FEATURED SCRIPTURE

As he who called you is holy, you also be holy in all your conduct, since it is written, "You shall be holy, for I am holy." . . . Conduct yourselves with fear throughout the time of your exile. —1 PETER 1:15-17

3 ACTIVITY OF THE DAY

Monday

How does it feel to be chosen by God as His own? What does it mean to be like Him, to be "holy"? In what ways are you acting as though you're *of* the world, not just *in* it?

_____

_____

_____

Tuesday

How does it feel to be planted in the world for now but not really be part of it? How do you respond to the hate or other abuse you receive for not being like unbelievers?

_____

_____

_____

Wednesday

Is your family, both as individual members and as a group, solely dedicated to serving God? Discuss this among yourselves. How can your family proclaim to society around you "the excellencies of him who called you out of darkness into his marvelous light"?

_____

_____

_____

Thursday

We are called to be witnesses for Christ while in this world. How can
we avoid being "unequally yoked" with unbelievers without placing
unnecessary barriers between us?

_____

_____

_____

_____

Friday

How should our new citizenship in heaven affect our citizenship in
the United States (or other nation)? Do you feel like an alien? Do you
long for a new country in a new heaven and earth? Discuss as a family
at dinner.

_____

_____

_____

_____

Saturday

What are some ways that your family acts differently from the world?
How hard does God want us to work at being holy? What sort of
person do you want to be by the time you appear before Him?

_____

_____

_____

_____

Sunday

Memorize this week's featured Bible passage or your favorite portion from one of the other readings.

4 CONCLUSION

We are strangers and aliens, no longer of this world but still in it for a time so that we may fulfill the assignments we're given to advance the kingdom. Our Lord has made it clear that He doesn't just want people who revere Him; He wants children who mirror His own holy character. But that won't happen without hard work on our part. We're commanded to *strive* for holiness, to be *diligent* in shedding the old nature. And the best way to do that is to rely on one another, especially in a family, where loved ones can identify the areas we need to improve on and support our efforts to change.

5 CLOSING PRAYER

Talk to God alone or together about your family, friends, church, and community, as well as about what He is saying to you today through His Word. Then conclude with this:

> *Holy, holy, holy, God of power and might. With our*
> *minds set on Your kingdom, we offer ourselves to You as*
> *living sacrifices. Sanctify us so that we might please You*
> *in all that we do and say. In Jesus's name. Amen.*

Warning Signals

"Not all who wander are lost"? It might depend on you.

1 OPENING PRAYER

Father, we've all been guilty of believing one thing while doing another. Whenever our conduct is not in step with the gospel, please call us back to You. In Jesus's name. Amen.

2 SCRIPTURE READING

Monday	PSALM 119:10-11, 37, 175-176; HEBREWS 3:12-14
Tuesday	DEUTERONOMY 29:18-19
Wednesday	2 CORINTHIANS 13:2-5; HEBREWS 12:1-2; 1 PETER 5:8-9
Thursday	GALATIANS 2:11-14; COLOSSIANS 1:28; 2 THESSALONIANS 3:14-15
Friday	PROVERBS 24:11; GALATIANS 5:19-21; 6:1; JAMES 5:19-20; JUDE 22-23
Saturday	1 JOHN 5:16
Sunday	1 THESSALONIANS 5:14

FEATURED SCRIPTURE

Him we proclaim, warning everyone and teaching everyone with all wisdom, that we may present everyone mature in Christ. —COLOSSIANS 1:28

3 ACTIVITY OF THE DAY

Monday

Do we, as Christians, still need to watch our steps from moment to moment? Or will righteous words and actions now just come naturally? Isn't it enough to be dedicated to biblical truth? Explain.

_____

_____

_____

_____

Tuesday

How might the sinful behavior of one family member affect the whole family? Or is it just "every man for himself"? Why?

_____

_____

_____

_____

Wednesday

How can you examine your own faith to see if you've strayed? What sins are still "clinging" to you? Consider asking others close to you what they think your weaknesses are.

_____

_____

_____

_____

_____

Thursday

As a couple, discuss whether anyone in your family is walking on shaky ground and needs a loving warning to change direction. Can you do this without making someone feel picked on? How?

_____

_____

_____

Friday

Has anyone in your immediate or extended family ever needed to be rescued from a destructive path? Explain. How was it done? Is God calling you to help rescue some other Christian you know?

_____

_____

_____

Saturday

Who in your family needs your prayers so that some sin of theirs can be defeated?

Sunday

Memorize this week's featured Bible passage or your favorite portion from one of the other readings.

4 CONCLUSION

The world, the flesh, and the devil are out to destroy you and your family. Count on it. But if we stay on guard for one another, we can defeat any attempt to deter us from the path to life. However uncomfortable it may seem, love demands that we warn, admonish, and sometimes snatch one another out of the fire so that we all make it to God's kingdom safely.

5 CLOSING PRAYER

Talk to God alone or together about your family, friends, church, and community, as well as about what He is saying to you today through His Word. Then conclude with this:

> *Lord, we all wander like sheep, but You are faithful to*
> *guide us back into the fold. Teach us to heed warnings*
> *when we fall into a wrong path, and help us admonish*
> *those You have given into our care. Amen.*

The Salt of the Earth

If we love only those who love us, what good is that?

1 OPENING PRAYER

Lord, You've called us to be the salt of the earth and the light of the world. Show us the meaning of Your words and what we must do to answer Your call. Amen.

2 SCRIPTURE READING

Monday	MATTHEW 5:13; MARK 9:42-50; LUKE 14:33-35
Tuesday	MATTHEW 5:14-16; JOHN 17:18; 1 TIMOTHY 6:17-19
Wednesday	MATTHEW 5:44-46; LUKE 6:27-36
Thursday	ACTS 5:14-16; JAMES 1:27
Friday	PHILIPPIANS 4:8
Saturday	COLOSSIANS 4:6; 1 PETER 3:13-17
Sunday	1 TIMOTHY 2:1-2

FEATURED SCRIPTURE

"Let your light shine before others, so that they may see your good works and give glory to your Father who is in heaven." —MATTHEW 5:16

3 ACTIVITY OF THE DAY

Monday

Under what conditions dare we expect to be used by God as a preservative and positive influence in society? Does your family have the "saltiness" it needs for such a mission? Explain.

_____

_____

_____

_____

Tuesday

Why shouldn't we ignore nonbelievers and concentrate only on meeting needs within the Christian community? What does God want your family to do for your neighbors? Discuss and pray about it together.

_____

_____

_____

_____

Wednesday

What is your attitude toward those who hate either you or Christians in general? What is God's attitude toward them? Why should your attitude be the same as the Lord's?

_____

_____

_____

_____

Thursday

What do Christians have that the world needs? As a family, try listing some areas of society (such as the media, arts, social services) that badly need Christians' involvement. Where do you feel called to join in?

_____

_____

_____

_____

Friday

Why shouldn't Christians confine their interests to the religious realm? What, if anything, does being the salt of the earth have to do with nature conservation, writing a fine novel, or cooking a delicious meal?

_____

_____

_____

Saturday

Describe in your own words the kind of speech or writing that is "seasoned with salt." How prepared are you to explain the gospel in a respectful and pleasing way?

_____

_____

_____

Sunday

Memorize this week's featured Bible passage or your favorite portion from one of the other readings.

4 CONCLUSION

Sometimes Christians have made the mistake of emphasizing social concern in lieu of personal holiness. But Jesus made it clear that we can't be the "salt" of the earth unless we maintain our own saltiness. We've also erroneously assumed that our only obligation to unbelievers is to preach the gospel, whereas Jesus sent us into the world to help with all sorts of human need. Just as He is kind to those who spurn Him, we are called to be like Him, loving those who hate us, speaking graciously to them, and praying for all.

5 CLOSING PRAYER

Talk to God alone or together about your family, friends, church, and community, as well as about what He is saying to you today through His Word. Then conclude with this:

Father, in Your amazing love You are kind to the
ungrateful and the evil, even as You were to us before
You called us to Yourself. Grant us the power to be like
You, reaching out in compassion to make life better for
friends and enemies alike. In Jesus's name. Amen.

Lie Detectors

Having been set apart by God, we must discern what is right and true.

1 OPENING PRAYER

Father, before You saved us we were darkened in our understanding and alienated from You. Now that we live in the light, show us how to cling to Your truth and no longer be fooled by the wisdom of this world. In Jesus's name. Amen.

2 SCRIPTURE READING

Monday	JOHN 8:42-44; ROMANS 1:28; EPHESIANS 4:17-18
Tuesday	ROMANS 1:29-32; 2 TIMOTHY 4:3-4
Wednesday	ACTS 20:29-32; GALATIANS 1:6-9; 2 PETER 2:1
Thursday	ROMANS 12:2A; 2 CORINTHIANS 7:1; EPHESIANS 5:6-10
Friday	EPHESIANS 4:14; COLOSSIANS 2:8; 2 PETER 3:14-18
Saturday	ROMANS 12:2B; 1 THESSALONIANS 5:21; 1 JOHN 4:1
Sunday	2 CORINTHIANS 10:4-5

See also JEREMIAH 29:8-9; 1 CORINTHIANS 1:18-20; 1 TIMOTHY 4:16

3 ACTIVITY OF THE DAY

Monday

What should we expect from people who walk "in the futility of their minds"? Why are we surprised by their worldview and behavior? Do we really believe that a person without God is lost, a captive of the devil?

_____

_____

_____

Tuesday

What are some examples in which our society not only tolerates but *approves of* false beliefs and immoral practices? How is the acceptance of lies evident in science, the media, education, or human behavior?

_____

_____

_____

Wednesday

Identify some of the religious heresies or false teachings that have been used to draw God's people away from the Lord. Who in your family or circle of friends has been taken in by such deceptions? Explain.

_____

_____

_____

_____

Thursday

How can we be renewed in mind and spirit, becoming less vulnerable to the lure of empty words? What do you do as a family to "discern what is pleasing to the Lord"?

_____

_____

_____

Friday

How would you like your kids to handle the daily onslaught of dubious messages and blatant lies? Describe how you study the Bible to make a right interpretation and not twist its meaning.

_____

_____

_____

Saturday

How can your family join together to discern and test what a family member is reading in a school textbook? Seeing at the movie theater or on the Web? Hearing in a newscast?

_____

_____

_____

Sunday

Memorize this week's featured Bible passage or your favorite portion from one of the other readings.

4 CONCLUSION

With the proliferation of media and information in this digital age, it's harder than ever before not to be swayed by the lies of the world. A barrage of deceptive messages begins to assault us as soon as we wake each morning. So we have to be proactive in letting God renew our minds. We can do this through rich exposure to His Word, wisdom in tuning out harmful media sources, and reliance on other Christians— especially those in our own family—to discern together what is right and true.

5 CLOSING PRAYER

Talk to God alone or together about your family, friends, church, and community, as well as about what He is saying to you today through His Word. Then conclude with this:

> *Jesus, we praise and thank You that we never again have to be tossed to and fro by the waves or carried about by every wind of doctrine, by human cunning. Keep us in Your boat, listening only to Your voice while the storm rages around us. Amen.*

Sound Teaching

We've been handed a treasure to share with others.

1 OPENING PRAYER

Lord, we worship You not only with our heart, soul, and strength, but also with our mind. Show us how to learn truth from You, so that we can then teach others. Amen.

2 SCRIPTURE READING

Monday	PROVERBS 9:9-10; 2 TIMOTHY 4:3-4; 2 JOHN 9-11
Tuesday	MATTHEW 28:19-20; 1 TIMOTHY 6:2-4
Wednesday	LUKE 10:38-42; ACTS 2:42
Thursday	DEUTERONOMY 6:4-7; ACTS 5:42; ROMANS 12:6-7; COLOSSIANS 3:16
Friday	PSALM 25:4-5; JOHN 7:16-18; 2 TIMOTHY 3:16
Saturday	2 TIMOTHY 1:13-14; TITUS 1:7-14; 2:1-8
Sunday	LUKE 19:47-48

See also ACTS 18:9-11; 2 TIMOTHY 2:24-25; REVELATION 2:14-16

FEATURED SCRIPTURE

"These words that I command you today shall be on your heart. You shall teach them diligently to your children, and shall talk of them when you sit in your house, and when you walk by the way, and when you lie down, and when you rise." —Deuteronomy 6:6-7

3 ACTIVITY OF THE DAY

Monday

Where do you start in trying to absorb sound teaching from the Lord? What matters more than intellectual curiosity or indoctrination?

_____

_____

_____

Tuesday

What is your overall purpose for instructing your children in the Christian faith? What is "teaching that accords with godliness"? How do you go about this?

_____

_____

_____

Wednesday

Are you and your family always "sitting at Jesus's feet," ready to be instructed? Or are you distracted by other things in life? How would you like to change your object of devotion?

_____

_____

_____

Thursday

While some Christians are specially gifted to teach in the church, all of us have been asked to teach our own children. Do you confine such teaching to certain occasions, or are you teaching them all day, every day? Why, and how?

_____

_____

_____

Friday

Who is your primary teacher these days—perhaps a pastor, Bible scholar, or author? Who was Jesus's teacher? Though we're called to teach one another, where must we go for most of our instruction? Are you hungry for such training?

_____

_____

_____

Saturday

Do you treasure the body of sound Christian doctrine that has been handed down to us? What are some of the most important biblical truths? Why do many believers today not know them? How can you ensure that your family is being fed by sound teaching?

_____

_____

_____

Sunday

Memorize this week's featured Bible passage or your favorite portion from one of the other readings.

4 CONCLUSION

Sadly, it's not uncommon today for a follower of Jesus to adopt religious and moral views based on what's accepted in the culture rather than looking to the Bible as the final authority. Biblical illiteracy and ignorance of sound Christian doctrine are widespread in the church. But you can, at least, counter this trend in your own family by systematically passing on the core of truths that make up a solid Christian worldview. Don't assume that your children are going to get this foundation from someone else. Make every moment a teaching moment.

5 CLOSING PRAYER

Talk to God alone or together about your family, friends, church, and community, as well as about what He is saying to you today through His Word. Then conclude with this:

> *Make us to know Your ways, O Lord; teach us Your*
> *paths. Lead us as a family in Your truth and teach us,*
> *for You are the God of our salvation. Amen.*

A Word of Advice

Who will help us apply what we've learned in Scripture?

1 OPENING PRAYER

Father, reveal to us the role of counselors in our lives, and keep us from trying to travel alone. In Jesus's name. Amen.

2 SCRIPTURE READING

Monday	PROVERBS 12:15; 19:20; ECCLESIASTES 4:13
Tuesday	PSALM 1:1
Wednesday	PSALM 73:24; JAMES 1:5
Thursday	PROVERBS 15:22; 20:18; 27:9
Friday	MATTHEW 28:18-20; TITUS 2:3-5
Saturday	PHILIPPIANS 3:17; TITUS 2:7-8
Sunday	PHILIPPIANS 4:9

FEATURED SCRIPTURE

The way of a fool is right in his own eyes, but a wise man listens to advice. —PROVERBS 12:15

3 ACTIVITY OF THE DAY

Monday

Where do you turn for counsel, or are you trying to navigate life on your own? Do your spouse and children ask you for spiritual and relational advice? Why or why not? How do you rate yourself as a listener?

_____

_____

_____

_____

Tuesday

Explain what's wrong with relying on the wisdom of non-Christian friends. Do your kids do this? Ask them whom they like to confide in, and why. What might be the advantage of having another mature Christian, other than their parents, disciple them on occasion?

_____

_____

_____

_____

Wednesday

Discuss as a family: When you need advice or counsel regarding a difficult decision, do you immediately turn to another person, or do you also quiet yourself before God and sincerely wait for Him to grant you wisdom? Explain.

_____

_____

_____

Thursday

What are some advantages of obtaining counsel from a *group* of advisers (such as your family) rather than just one? Do you have regular family meetings where this can happen? Why or why not?

_____

_____

_____

Friday

Why did Jesus send His eleven disciples out to make "disciples" (not just believers) of all nations, "teaching them *to observe* all that I have commanded you" rather than "teaching them all that I have commanded you"?

_____

_____

_____

Saturday

How much of discipling has to do with offering verbal advice, and how much is being an example to follow? In what areas do you need to become a better role model for your family?

_____

_____

_____

Sunday

Memorize this week's featured Bible passage or your favorite portion from one of the other readings.

4 CONCLUSION

In some church traditions, Christians seek out older, wiser mentors who offer to disciple them. Others turn to professional counselors for help in crises. Most of us, however, just rely on a friend or two for occasional advice. The family is a rich source of counsel that we occasionally tend to overlook. When several people who know us well and care for us weigh in on a dilemma we're facing, we not only get to see the problem from several vantage points, but the interplay between family members adds even more insight. Don't discount the value of input from children; sometimes they can be the smartest people in the room.

5 CLOSING PRAYER

Talk to God alone or together about your family, friends, church, and community, as well as about what He is saying to you today through His Word. Then conclude with this:

> *Give us wisdom, O Father, not only for ourselves but for those*
> *You would have us counsel, so that we may more fully glorify*
> *You in all that we do and say. In Jesus's name. Amen.*

Everyone Plays a Part

As each has received a gift, use it to serve one another.

1 OPENING PRAYER

Lord, show us how we were meant to complement one another in the church and in the family, so that much can be accomplished for You by working together. Amen.

2 SCRIPTURE READING

Monday	NEHEMIAH 3:1-7; 4:15-17; ROMANS 12:4-5
Tuesday	1 CORINTHIANS 12:4-11; 14:26
Wednesday	1 CORINTHIANS 3:5-8; 15:10
Thursday	1 CORINTHIANS 12:21-25
Friday	EPHESIANS 4:15-16; COLOSSIANS 2:18-19
Saturday	1 PETER 4:10-11
Sunday	EPHESIANS 4:4-7

FEATURED SCRIPTURE

For as in one body we have many members, and the members do not all have the same function, so we, though many, are one body in Christ, and individually members one of another. —ROMANS 12:4-5

3 ACTIVITY OF THE DAY

Monday

What would our world be like if all flowers were red, or every season had the same weather as the rest of the year? What would your family be like if every member had the same skills, interests, calling, and personality? Why did God make us all different?

_____

_____

_____

_____

Tuesday

Ask your children why they think God gave them a special interest or skill or way of looking at things. How can our unique gifts serve the good of the whole family?

_____

_____

_____

_____

Wednesday

Don't you deserve a little credit for the good things you accomplish? Why do we give special praise to actors, athletes, authors, singers, and other people in the public eye? How should we each view our own achievements?

_____

_____

_____

Thursday

What will determine whether each of us succeeds in fulfilling the assignments God has given us? Do you really think you *need* your spouse and/or children? Why or why not?

_____

_____

_____

_____

Friday

How well do Paul's descriptions of the church also portray what your family is like? What, ultimately, holds your family together?

_____

_____

_____

_____

Saturday

Why do we often use our distinctive talents to compete with one another rather than serve one another? Whose glory do you really long for?

_____

_____

_____

Sunday

Memorize this week's featured Bible passage or your favorite portion from one of the other readings.

4 CONCLUSION

Remember when your family last gathered around the table to assemble a jigsaw puzzle? Every member helped find and join the pieces together, then what emerged was a beautiful picture. That's how God intends the family to work. We all make our unique contribution, we all follow His call on our lives, and the result is a powerful body of believers with Christ as the Head. So we should relish the chance to use our gifts for the common good and the glory of God. No one in the family is unessential.

5 CLOSING PRAYER

Talk to God alone or together about your family, friends, church, and community, as well as about what He is saying to you today through His Word. Then conclude with this:

> *Father, as we each do our part for the kingdom, help us grow*
> *up in every way into Him who is the Head, into Christ, who*
> *makes the body build itself up in love. For Your glory. Amen.*

Your Household and God's

Your family needs the church, and the church needs your family.

1 OPENING PRAYER

Lord, thank You for bringing us into Your family, the church. This week, show us how our own family can be a vital part of the whole household of God. In Your name. Amen.

2 SCRIPTURE READING

Monday	ACTS 2:46-47; 5:42
Tuesday	ACTS 11:13-14; 18:8
Wednesday	ACTS 16:25-34
Thursday	ROMANS 16:3-5; 1 CORINTHIANS 16:15-19; COLOSSIANS 4:15
Friday	EPHESIANS 2:19-22
Saturday	PHILEMON 1-3
Sunday	1 TIMOTHY 3:14-15

FEATURED SCRIPTURE

And day by day, attending the temple together and breaking bread in their homes, they received their food with glad and generous hearts, praising God and having favor with all the people. —ACTS 2:46-47

3 ACTIVITY OF THE DAY

Monday

What do you think of the fact that, right from the start, the church used both larger gatherings in public and smaller gatherings in people's homes to worship and fulfill its mission? Does your home serve as part of the church?

_____

_____

_____

Tuesday

In the New Testament, often an entire household turned to the Lord at once. Why does this sound strange to modern ears? Do you think of your walk with the Lord mostly as a private, individual affair, or have you embraced the concept of following Him together as a group?

_____

_____

_____

Wednesday

Imagine the impact that Paul and Silas had on the jailer's children (Acts 16). How would your own kids benefit from knowing and relating to other mature Christian adults, not just to Mom and Dad?

_____

_____

Thursday

Do you think of your church and your household as two fairly separate institutions? Why or why not? Were they always that distinct? Should they be? Have you talked to any Christians who are involved in a house church today? If so, what did you learn?

_____

_____

_____

_____

Friday

Why did the apostle Paul describe the church as the "household of God," a place where the Lord can dwell and call home? How can you help make church meetings feel more like family gatherings, where people get to know one another intimately?

_____

_____

_____

Saturday

As a family, decide whether there's another family in your church that God would want you to reach out to, family-to-family. Don't forget to consider single-parent homes that would especially appreciate your friendship.

_____

_____

_____

_____

Sunday

Memorize this week's featured Bible passage or your favorite portion from one of the other readings.

4 CONCLUSION

How much of the New Testament offers instructions regarding church programs, facilities, Sunday school, worship services, sermons, or clergy training? On the other hand, how much of it deals with everyday relationships between believers? (Hint: Review the table of contents in this book.) Ultimately, what did Jesus have in mind when He said He was going to build His church? If relationships are central to the church's mission and identity, then where are those relationships more critical than in the family, which is a microcosm of the larger fellowship? We should never expect the institutional church to do for us what the Lord wants us to do first in our own homes.

5 CLOSING PRAYER

Talk to God alone or together about your family, friends, church, and community, as well as about what He is saying to you today through His Word. Then conclude with this:

> _O God, let us be a dwelling place for You, so that whether we are at home or out in society, our words and actions serve to make Your glorious presence known. In Jesus's name. Amen._

Proclaim the Gospel

Does your family have the aroma of Christ?

1 OPENING PRAYER

Lord Jesus, by Your Spirit make us powerful witnesses for You, so that the world may come to know You and give glory to Your Father in heaven. Amen.

2 SCRIPTURE READING

Monday	JOHN 6:44; ACTS 1:8; 2 CORINTHIANS 4:3-4
Tuesday	MATTHEW 5:14-16
Wednesday	MATTHEW 10:42; 25:35-40; JAMES 2:15-16; 1 JOHN 3:17-18
Thursday	1 PETER 3:15-16
Friday	JOHN 13:33-35; 17:20-23; 2 CORINTHIANS 2:15-16
Saturday	2 CORINTHIANS 5:19-20; 1 JOHN 1:1-3
Sunday	1 THESSALONIANS 2:2-4

FEATURED SCRIPTURE

"By this all people will know that you are my disciples, if you have love for one another." —JOHN 13:35

3 ACTIVITY OF THE DAY

Monday

Have you ever tried to convince someone to accept Christ? If so, did you feel pressure to succeed in it? What is our role in proclaiming the gospel, and what is God's? Why? How does intercessory prayer come into play?

_____

_____

_____

Tuesday

Is your church or family shedding light on the surrounding community? How so? Why are Christians often inconspicuous, not just in a particular locale, but in the media and culture? What contacts do you maintain with non-Christians?

_____

_____

_____

Wednesday

What has evangelism to do with meeting people's immediate, felt needs? If what unbelievers really need is to be saved and come to know Jesus, why would your family bother with "social action"?

_____

_____

Thursday

How prepared are you "to make a defense to anyone who asks you for a reason for the hope that is in you"? What are you doing to grasp where most people are coming from today? In your family, practice trying to articulate the basic gospel message to one another.

_____

_____

_____

Friday

What did Jesus say is the primary way we can be His witnesses and draw people to Him? What are some ways they might see our unity and love for one another? Or do we not act or live much differently from the rest of the world, so there's nothing to see?

_____

_____

_____

Saturday

Do you often implore people to give their lives to Christ? Why or why not? Write out your personal testimony and practice saying it. Finally, ask family members how each of them feels about telling others of Jesus. What parts make them uncomfortable?

_____

_____

_____

Sunday

Memorize this week's featured Bible passage or your favorite portion from one of the other readings.

4 CONCLUSION

Everyone in your family should feel some responsibility for helping others encounter Jesus Christ—the Way, the Truth, and the Life. But "personal evangelism" is only one of the means by which we act as witnesses for the Lord. People will know that Jesus is real, and that following Him is the path to an entirely new existence, if they see how deeply Christians love one another (John 13:35). Jesus had in mind a kind of love that the world knows nothing of and that sadly is often missing among believers. It's a love acted out by the many "one another" commands discussed in this devotional guide. And that's why a Christian family has a better chance to proclaim the gospel than any individual will ever have. Jesus's message to families is simple: "People will know that you are My disciples if you have love for one another."

5 CLOSING PRAYER

Talk to God alone or together about your family, friends, church, and community, as well as about what He is saying to you today through His Word. Then conclude with this:

Father, You have filled us with the assurance that we will live together with You. Use us to bring others into Your family as well. And remind us of our glorious future whenever we are slandered for extolling Your name. In Jesus's name we pray. Amen.

A Little Respect

Why Christians should have favor with all the people

1 OPENING PRAYER

Father, show us how to conduct ourselves so that we are never an obstacle to those who might turn their lives over to You. In Jesus's name. Amen.

2 SCRIPTURE READING

Monday	ACTS 2:45-47; 4:14, 18-21; 5:12-14
Tuesday	1 CORINTHIANS 10:32-33; 2 CORINTHIANS 8:20-21; TITUS 2:7-8
Wednesday	COLOSSIANS 4:5
Thursday	1 TIMOTHY 3:1-7
Friday	TITUS 3:1-2
Saturday	1 THESSALONIANS 4:10-12
Sunday	1 PETER 2:12-15

FEATURED SCRIPTURE

We aim at what is honorable not only in the Lord's sight but also in the sight of man. —2 CORINTHIANS 8:21

3 ACTIVITY OF THE DAY

Monday

Why did the early Christians in Jerusalem have favor with the populace? Are Christians viewed favorably by unbelievers today? Why or why not?

_____

_____

_____

_____

Tuesday

Why does the New Testament say it is important for Christians to make a favorable impression on people in general? How is your family viewed by neighbors, unsaved friends, and relatives?

_____

_____

_____

_____

Wednesday

To review, describe how you should speak to outsiders about your faith. What sort of talk turns people away from the gospel?

_____

_____

_____

_____

Thursday

Throughout the apostle Paul's first letter to Timothy, he is concerned that Christians maintain a good reputation in the community. Why is it especially important that Christian leaders be above reproach?

_____

_____

_____

_____

Friday

Do you and your family "speak evil of no one" and show "perfect courtesy toward all people" no matter how negative someone's influence may be on the nation, the church, or your loved ones? Explain. What good work can your family do to win favor with your neighbors?

_____

_____

_____

_____

Saturday

What else does Paul say is important as part of "walking properly before outsiders"?

_____

_____

_____

_____

Sunday

Memorize this week's featured Bible passage or your favorite portion from one of the other readings.

4 CONCLUSION

As aliens living in hostile territory, we walk a fine line. Jesus warned us to expect persecution for our loyalty to Him, yet we must do everything we can to maintain favor with outsiders, so that when we are disparaged, it is not a response to anything we did or said to offend needlessly. Unbelievers should have "nothing evil to say about us." We must concentrate on doing good to all people, so that they might appreciate our positive impact on their lives.

5 CLOSING PRAYER

Talk to God alone or together about your family, friends, church, and community, as well as about what He is saying to you today through His Word. Then conclude with this:

> *Lord, help us to walk in wisdom toward*
> *outsiders, so that many of them may see You*
> *in us and come to You for eternal life. Amen.*

Band of Brothers (and Sisters)

Striving side by side, fight the good fight of the faith.

1 OPENING PRAYER

Lord, give us courage to face the battle we find ourselves in, so we can be faithful soldiers in Your service till the war is won. Amen.

2 SCRIPTURE READING

Monday	EPHESIANS 6:12; 1 TIMOTHY 6:12; 2 TIMOTHY 2:4
Tuesday	ROMANS 13:12-14; 2 CORINTHIANS 6:1-7
Wednesday	EPHESIANS 6:13-18; 1 THESSALONIANS 5:8
Thursday	PHILIPPIANS 1:27-28
Friday	2 CORINTHIANS 6:8-10; 2 TIMOTHY 2:3; 1 PETER 4:1-2
Saturday	ROMANS 16:20; REVELATION 12:11-12
Sunday	2 CORINTHIANS 10:4-5

See also HEBREWS 11:32-34; JUDE 3

FEATURED SCRIPTURE

Take up the whole armor of God, that you may be able to withstand in the evil day, and having done all, to stand firm. —EPHESIANS 6:13

3 ACTIVITY OF THE DAY

Monday

Do you see yourself not as one living a "normal life," but as a soldier commissioned to wage cosmic war against the spiritual forces of evil? Explain. How deeply entangled are you in civilian pursuits?

_____

_____

_____

Tuesday

What does it mean to "put on the Lord Jesus Christ"? Why is personal righteousness critical for the battle we're engaged in? What can we accomplish for God if we are still held back by the "flesh"?

_____

_____

_____

Wednesday

Have you and your family members taken up the _whole_ armor of God? In what areas is your family weak or unprotected? What will you do about it? How effective are you at wielding your sword, the Word of God?

_____

_____

_____

Thursday

What are you doing to make sure your family members are striving for the faith *side by side,* not as solo warriors in a losing battle? How are you all joining forces with other Christians around the world?

_____

_____

_____

_____

Friday

Do you really expect to suffer as a soldier of Christ Jesus? If we aren't suffering now, why? What should we prepare for in the future? As a family, how do you respond to the persecution of Christians in other countries?

_____

_____

_____

_____

Saturday

How does it help to know that victory is certain, and not far off? What are some positive signs that the gospel is making gains around the world?

_____

_____

_____

_____

Sunday

Memorize this week's featured Bible passage or your favorite portion from one of the other readings.

4 CONCLUSION

When a man is called into military service overseas, all thoughts of a normal, peaceful life are abandoned. Gone are his dreams of a summer vacation at the beach, or a white Christmas just like the ones he used to know. Likewise, we must abandon our pursuit of a comfortable existence, the American dream, or whatever false hope we have about this present life. Good times are coming soon, but meanwhile we have to don the armor that God has given us and be willing to go into battle every day. Fortunately, we have one another to rely on in the trenches, so there's no need to be a lone hero. With God's help, make your family the boldest squad in the army!

5 CLOSING PRAYER

Talk to God alone or together about your family, friends, church, and community, as well as about what He is saying to you today through His Word. Then conclude with this:

> *Since we belong to the day, O Father, let us be sober, having put on the breastplate of righteousness, and for a helmet the hope of salvation. All to Your glory. Amen.*

Deliver Us from Evil

Watch out for it, abhor it, cast it off, put it away.

1 OPENING PRAYER

Lord, make us hate evil as much as You do, whether it's inside us or in the world. Give us victory over temptation. For Your glory. Amen.

2 SCRIPTURE READING

Monday	PSALM 97:10; 119:127-128; AMOS 5:15; ROMANS 12:9
Tuesday	ROMANS 13:12-14; EPHESIANS 4:22-24; JAMES 1:21; 1 PETER 2:1
Wednesday	1 CORINTHIANS 10:12-13; GALATIANS 6:1
Thursday	MATTHEW 4:1-11
Friday	MATTHEW 26:40-41
Saturday	HEBREWS 4:14-16; 12:1-2
Sunday	COLOSSIANS 3:8-10

FEATURED SCRIPTURE

Let us also lay aside every weight, and sin which clings so closely, and let us run with endurance the race that is set before us, looking to Jesus, the founder and perfecter of our faith. —HEBREWS 12:1-2

3 ACTIVITY OF THE DAY

Monday

What is so despicable about evil? Do you have the same reaction to sin that our Lord does, or do you find yourself getting used to—even passively accepting—the sin you see every day, whether in society or in yourself?

_____

_____

_____

Tuesday

The Bible uses strong words to describe how we should cease our former practices. What specific sins call for more intense efforts on your part to fling them away? How can the family help each of us "put off the old self"?

_____

_____

_____

Wednesday

Do you think you're immune to certain kinds of temptation? Explain. Why is it important to keep watch on ourselves? Again, how can loved ones be on guard for us so that we don't wander off the path?

_____

_____

Thursday

Describe how you use Scripture to fight against temptation. How would a better grasp of the Bible, even memorizing key passages, help you avoid sin and bring glory to God?

_____

_____

_____

Friday

Discuss as a couple or family: When you're under spiritual attack, how important is prayer? Why do you need God's help? Are you willing to wait for an hour or more to hear His voice or find His peace? Explain.

_____

_____

_____

_____

Saturday

When we feel too weak to face trials or fight off temptation, how does it help to look to Jesus for an example? Or to former heroes of the faith, who endured even more than we are facing?

_____

_____

_____

_____

Sunday

Memorize this week's featured Bible passage or your favorite portion from one of the other readings.

4 CONCLUSION

We're like the proverbial frogs being slowly boiled alive. So much evil assaults us every day, whether on the street, in the news, or at work, that we start to get used to it. What was abhorrent just a few years ago is now tolerated, if not praised. Even with ourselves, we tend to accept our faults and sinful ways rather than being offended by them. But the New Testament will have none of that. "Hate it! Fling it away!" cries the apostle Paul. "Make *no* provision for the flesh" (Romans 13:14, emphasis added). "Clean house!" says the apostle Peter. "Make a clean sweep of malice and pretense, envy and hurtful talk" (1 Peter 2:1, *The Message*, a paraphrase). We have to identify exactly what we're doing that displeases God, then aggressively put a stop to it. But, of course, we will succeed only with help from Scripture, prayer, and the example of others, whether from the past or from our own family members, who must keep us accountable.

5 CLOSING PRAYER

Talk to God alone or together about your family, friends, church, and community, as well as about what He is saying to you today through His Word. Then conclude with this:

Lead us not into temptation, but deliver us from evil. For Yours is the kingdom and the power and the glory, forever. Amen.

Intercede for One Another

Praying as a family is good, but intercession is critical!

1 OPENING PRAYER

Father, never let it be said that we don't have because we didn't ask You. Teach us how to pray for one another in a way that glorifies Your name. Amen.

2 SCRIPTURE READING

Monday	MATTHEW 7:7-11; JAMES 4:2-3
Tuesday	JOHN 14:12-14; 15:16; 16:23-24
Wednesday	ACTS 4:23-31; 2 CORINTHIANS 1:8-11; 2 THESSALONIANS 3:1-2
Thursday	EPHESIANS 1:15-21; 3:14-19; COLOSSIANS 1:9-12
Friday	1 CORINTHIANS 1:4-8; 2 THESSALONIANS 1:3
Saturday	EPHESIANS 6:18-20; COLOSSIANS 4:12; 2 THESSALONIANS 1:11-12
Sunday	HEBREWS 13:20-21

See also JAMES 5:16; 1 JOHN 5:14-16; JUDE 20-21

FEATURED SCRIPTURE

We always pray for you, that our God may make you worthy of his calling and may fulfill every resolve for good and every work of faith by his power, so that the name of our Lord Jesus may be glorified in you.

—2 THESSALONIANS 1:11-12

3 ACTIVITY OF THE DAY

Monday

What are some things you long to see happen for a loved one but rarely remember to ask God about? Why don't you ask? What, if anything, makes you uncertain of the Lord's willingness to grant your wishes for that person?

_____

_____

Tuesday

Given the context of today's verses, what did Jesus mean when He told us to pray "in my [His] name"? Do you do this? What is Jesus's primary motivation for answering such prayers? (See John 14:13.)

_____

_____

Wednesday

Do you pray for one another's well-being and success in life, or do you pray more that God's kingdom will be advanced through one another? Why? Does it matter? What really drives you to prayer?

_____

_____

Thursday

While it's fine to pray for a person's health, job interview, travel safety, etc., what should be the real focus of our prayers for one another? Using one of the prayers in today's readings, intercede for a family member.

_____

_____

_____

Friday

Pause today and offer thanks to God for each member of your family. Tell Him what pleases you about them, and thank Him for what He is doing in their lives. Consider asking the whole family to pray this way conversationally together.

_____

_____

_____

Saturday

How faithful are you in "praying at all times in the Spirit," always on the alert to intercede for Christians everywhere? If you aren't doing well at this, why? What do you consider a better use of your time?

_____

_____

Sunday

Memorize this week's featured Bible passage or your favorite portion
from one of the other readings.

4 CONCLUSION

If the apostle Paul sat in on a small group prayer meeting today,
would he be perplexed by the content of our prayers? How often do
we go beyond the usual health and financial requests to ask for deeper
things, such as a person's grasp of the hope to which God has called
us, or the strength to comprehend more fully the love of Christ that
surpasses knowledge? Why do we plead for tough situations to go
away rather than praying that the gospel will be advanced through
our sufferings? But if we ask according to God's will, if we ask in
Jesus's name, there's nothing our Lord won't do. "Ask away!" He has
said over and over. Ask Him for good things in your family, and ask
Him to sustain fellow believers who are suffering in Syria. Ask at all
times of the day, taking your role as intercessor more seriously than
anything else on your agenda. Help your own family become a team
of intercessors with global and eternal impact.

5 CLOSING PRAYER

Talk to God alone or together about your family, friends, church, and
community, as well as about what He is saying to you today through
His Word. Then conclude with this:

> *Jesus, help us always to struggle on one another's behalf
> in our prayers, so that we all may stand mature and
> fully assured in the will of Your Father. Amen.*

Hard Times

*"If they persecuted me,
they will also persecute
you." —Jesus*

1 OPENING PRAYER

Lord, You suffered death in order to bring us eternal life. Make us
ready and willing to suffer with You, knowing that the reward for our
patience will be great. Amen.

2 SCRIPTURE READING

Monday	JOHN 15:19-20; ROMANS 8:16-17; 1 PETER 2:20-23
Tuesday	1 CORINTHIANS 4:10-13; HEBREWS 10:32-36; JAMES 1:2
Wednesday	2 CORINTHIANS 4:8-11; 12:10; PHILIPPIANS 1:29-30
Thursday	1 CORINTHIANS 12:26; 2 CORINTHIANS 11:28-29; HEBREWS 13:3
Friday	1 THESSALONIANS 3:1-5; 2 TIMOTHY 3:10-13; 1 PETER 4:12-14
Saturday	2 CORINTHIANS 4:16-18; 1 PETER 1:3-9
Sunday	HEBREWS 12:3-4

See also 1 THESSALONIANS 2:14-16; 1 PETER 3:17

FEATURED SCRIPTURE

Beloved, do not be surprised at the fiery trial when it comes upon you to test you, as though something strange were happening to you. But rejoice insofar as you share Christ's sufferings, that you may also rejoice and be glad when his glory is revealed. —1 PETER 4:12-13

3 ACTIVITY OF THE DAY

Monday

The New Testament seems to say that we can't follow Jesus without being persecuted. Have you suffered for Him? If we don't suffer with Him, what happens? How do you feel about having an easier life than Jesus had?

_____

_____

Tuesday

How should a Christian respond to hostility? Would you, or do you, react in that way? Based on today's readings, how should we pray for our brothers and sisters around the world who are being persecuted?

_____

_____

Wednesday

Do you owe Jesus anything? What are you willing to endure for His sake? Have there been times when you would have suffered for Him if you had spoken up, but you chose to remain silent? Explain.

_____

_____

Thursday

If we ourselves aren't suffering much for Christ, why should our pain still be just as deep as if we were? As a family, discuss how you can identify with and support Christians overseas who are under persecution.

_____

_____

_____

Friday

If we aren't being persecuted now, should we be surprised if that changes in the future? What happens if persecution begins when we didn't expect or prepare for it?

_____

_____

_____

Saturday

How can our expectation of the glorious life to come help us consider severe suffering in this present life to be nothing more than "light momentary affliction"? What excites you about your future as a child of God?

_____

_____

Sunday

Memorize this week's featured Bible passage or your favorite portion from one of the other readings.

4 CONCLUSION

For most Christians in America, it's startling to hear the Bible say that accepting Jesus as Lord is a guaranteed path to persecution. Jesus said so, as did Paul, Peter, and others. But most of us just haven't experienced any real suffering, while our brothers and sisters in many parts of the world are being tried by fire. So what shall we do? First, we must expect persecution to come, so that we aren't surprised when it does. Second, we should take Paul seriously when he wrote, "If one member suffers, all suffer together." We are called to bear the pain that our fellow believers are going through—by praying for them, writing to them, and advocating for justice whenever we can. Finally, we must not duck when we have an opportunity to speak up for Jesus, despite the scorn that will be heaped on us for our witness.

5 CLOSING PRAYER

Talk to God alone or together about your family, friends, church, and community, as well as about what He is saying to you today through His Word. Then conclude with this:

Though we have not seen You, we love You. Though we do not now see You, we believe in You and rejoice with joy that is inexpressible, obtaining the outcome of our faith, the salvation of our souls. Thank You, Lord. Amen.

Growing Old Gracefully

Biblical advice to family members who've been traveling long

1 OPENING PRAYER

Lord, as we approach our senior years, we praise You that we have life eternal, and that death is not the end but a beginning. Show us how to glorify You while we are still in these bodies. Amen.

2 SCRIPTURE READING

Monday	PSALM 39:4-6; 90:10-12; ROMANS 13:11
Tuesday	PSALM 71:9-14; LUKE 14:26-30; ACTS 20:24
Wednesday	ECCLESIASTES 12:1-7; COLOSSIANS 1:11-12
Thursday	PHILIPPIANS 4:11-13; 1 TIMOTHY 6:6-8
Friday	2 THESSALONIANS 1:11-12; 3:11-12
Saturday	PSALM 50:23; PROVERBS 15:13-15; 17:22; ECCLESIASTES 3:11-12; 8:15; HEBREWS 12:28
Sunday	2 TIMOTHY 4:7-8

FEATURED SCRIPTURE

I have fought the good fight, I have finished the race, I have kept the faith. Henceforth there is laid up for me the crown of righteousness, which the Lord, the righteous judge, will award to me on that Day, and not only to me but also to all who have loved his appearing. —2 TIMOTHY 4:7-8

3 ACTIVITY OF THE DAY

Monday

Does it surprise you that a big part of your "toil and trouble" in this present life is over? What are your goals for your remaining years? How do you want to prepare for meeting Jesus face-to-face?

_____

_____

_____

Tuesday

What reward is there for a runner who quits before reaching the finish line? Are you strong in your faith, or are doubts and disappointments creeping in to tarnish your relationship with God? What will you do about it?

_____

_____

_____

Wednesday

The writer of Ecclesiastes drew a depressing picture of the debilitating aspects of aging. How well are you coping with the loss of your youthful abilities, and how can you become more patient, even in the midst of pain?

_____

_____

_____

_____

Thursday

Are you ready to be content financially, no matter what happens when living on a fixed income? How did the apostle Paul find such contentment?

_____

_____

_____

Friday

Whether you are employed or not, what is your plan for continuing to do "good work" as a senior? Why is it important not to "walk in idleness" during your so-called retirement years?

_____

_____

_____

Saturday

Despite the trials we face late in life, how will you avoid becoming a grouch or complainer? Why should we be thankful? What are some of the benefits of a cheerful heart?

_____

_____

Sunday

Memorize this week's featured Bible passage or your favorite portion from one of the other readings.

4 CONCLUSION

Old age brings physical, emotional, and financial challenges, but they should be overshadowed by gratitude for a life lived and joy in what is yet to come, especially seeing Jesus and rejoining loved ones in heaven. It's important not to quit the race prematurely or do anything that spoils our witness for God. People will not remember who we were at age 20, but they *will* remember what kind of people we were when the chips were down in our later years. We must do our best not to be a burden to our family members, whether emotionally or financially. Since retirement is not a biblical notion, we can show our dedication to the Lord by continuing to work for Him in some capacity till the end. Intercessory prayer is a great way to have an impact on the kingdom, even for those who can't leave the house.

5 CLOSING PRAYER

Talk to God alone or together about your family, friends, church, and community, as well as about what He is saying to you today through His Word. Then conclude with this:

> *Father, our salvation is nearer to us now than when we first believed. Help us to finish the race, to keep the faith, so we may enter Your kingdom and praise You forever. Amen.*

Generation to Generation

Our assignment extends to our children's children and beyond.

1 OPENING PRAYER

Our Father, lift our eyes for a moment beyond our immediate families and teach us to care for the generations that will come after. Then show us what we can do today to pass on the faith. Amen.

2 SCRIPTURE READING

Monday	DEUTERONOMY 4:9-10; 6:1-7; PSALM 48:12-14
Tuesday	1 SAMUEL 2:26; 8:1-3; 2 KINGS 20:2-3, 16-18, 21; 21:1-3
Wednesday	2 TIMOTHY 1:5
Thursday	PSALM 78:1-4; 2 TIMOTHY 2:1-2
Friday	2 TIMOTHY 3:14-15
Saturday	2 PETER 1:12-15
Sunday	PSALM 103:15-17

FEATURED SCRIPTURE

*We will . . . tell to the coming generation
the glorious deeds of the Lord, and his might,
and the wonders that he has done.* —PSALM 78:4

3 ACTIVITY OF THE DAY

Monday

What measures are you taking to make sure that your children *and grandchildren* know the Lord? Describe the methods you've found most effective for training young children in the ways of God.

_____

_____

_____

Tuesday

How might/does it feel to have one's children turn away from Christ? How can you help prevent such a tragedy, or what can you do if it has already happened? What is your deepest prayer for your children?

_____

_____

_____

Wednesday

Were you and/or your spouse raised in a Christian home? Were your parents? If so, what impact has that rich heritage had on you? If not, how would you like to establish such a tradition of faith for your family line?

_____

_____

_____

Thursday

Describe your role not just in helping your children and grandchildren find God but in preserving the faith for subsequent generations. How can you strengthen the church that will be here long after you go to heaven?

_____

_____

_____

Friday

Are you a good model of someone who is always and deeply immersed in the Word of God? What are some creative ways you can impart this same passion to your family members?

_____

_____

_____

Saturday

If you've raised your children in the Lord, is your job done? Why is it important to constantly "stir up" the commitment that a loved one has already made to Christ? How can you do this, even with grown children?

_____

_____

_____

Sunday

Memorize this week's featured Bible passage or your favorite portion from one of the other readings.

4 CONCLUSION

Life is a relay race, where the best runners take a firm hold of the baton handed to them and then ensure that it is passed safely on to those who follow after. Each family inherits a legacy and either safeguards it or amends it as needed so that not just the children, but many generations to come, enjoy rich spiritual blessings. But there is a mystery here: Why do some children not live by the gospel they were raised in? In the much-quoted Proverbs 22:6, does God promise a happy outcome for all Christian parents who did their best? Whatever the answer is, we at least know this: We are called to do our part and to pray ceaselessly, perhaps the rest of our lives, for the children and grandchildren we love so much. We cannot do better than to leave them in God's hands.

5 CLOSING PRAYER

Talk to God alone or together about your family, friends, church, and community, as well as about what He is saying to you today through His Word. Then conclude with this:

> *Lord, we and our children and grandchildren want to
> be people who talk of You when we sit in our house, and
> when we walk by the way, and when we lie down, and
> when we rise. Let it be all for Your glory. Amen.*

Lay Down Your Life

We are called to die for one another.

1 OPENING PRAYER

Lord, once again You set the example for us all. Help us grasp the
hard truths in this lesson, then give us the power to do as told. Amen.

2 SCRIPTURE READING

Monday	JOHN 10:11; 15:13; PHILIPPIANS 2:5-8; 1 JOHN 3:16
Tuesday	JOHN 12:24-26; 13:37-38; PHILIPPIANS 2:19-21; 2 TIMOTHY 4:9-10
Wednesday	ROMANS 16:3-4; 1 CORINTHIANS 15:30-31; 2 CORINTHIANS 1:6; PHILIPPIANS 2:29-30
Thursday	ROMANS 8:35-37
Friday	2 CORINTHIANS 12:15; 1 THESSALONIANS 2:8
Saturday	PHILIPPIANS 2:17; COLOSSIANS 1:24
Sunday	2 TIMOTHY 2:10

FEATURED SCRIPTURE

*By this we know love, that he laid down his life for us, and we ought to
lay down our lives for the brothers.* — 1 JOHN 3:16

3 ACTIVITY OF THE DAY

Monday

Why is merely being grateful for Christ's sacrificial death not enough? In what ways do you want to be like Jesus? In what ways would you rather *not* have to follow Him?

_____

_____

_____

_____

Tuesday

What did Jesus mean by "whoever loves his life"? Do you love yours? If you were to give it up anew, how would it be different? Do we have the strength to lay down our lives on our own? Explain.

_____

_____

_____

_____

Wednesday

How should family members lay down their lives for one another? Talk about it together and make a list of everyday, practical ways we can die to self and live for others. Do any of them involve risk?

_____

_____

_____

_____

Thursday

How can knowing deeply the love of Christ set us free to lay down our lives for others, even to the point of death? Read some testimonies from persecuted Christians, past or present.

_____

_____

_____

Friday

Why should the family be the one place where it's easiest to "die" for others? What drove the apostle Paul to expend himself for the welfare of fellow believers?

_____

_____

_____

Saturday

When you give up your own time, needs, or resources to bless another, how does it feel (even in small things like letting someone merge into your traffic lane)? Why did God make joy a part of every sacrificial act?

_____

_____

_____

_____

Sunday

Memorize this week's featured Bible passage or your favorite portion
from one of the other readings.

4 CONCLUSION

Some of the most moving stories on film portray the main character
literally giving up his or her life to save others. The astronaut detaches
himself from the tether so that his space-walking companion might
survive. The hobbit faces certain death on a perilous mission to save
Middle Earth. The mom succumbs in the hospital bed so her new-
born child can live. But laying down one's life often isn't so dramatic.
Merely being a good spouse or parent requires us to die every day—to
die to our own needs and desires so we can invest more time and
energy in those we love. No death, whether the ultimate kind or the
smallest sacrifice, comes easy. We must look to Jesus for an example
and for His help in our struggle to lose our life so we can gain it.

5 CLOSING PRAYER

Talk to God alone or together about your family, friends, church, and
community, as well as about what He is saying to you today through
His Word. Then conclude with this:

> *Father, since nothing can separate us from the love of Christ,*
> *we have nothing to lose. Set us free to lay down our lives, both*
> *in the home and wherever You lead us. In Jesus's name. Amen.*

What Time Is It?

All the world's a stage, and this is the final act.

1 OPENING PRAYER

Lord, help us to interpret the time we live in, so that we can make the best use of our remaining days. All for Your glory. Amen.

2 SCRIPTURE READING

Monday	ECCLESIASTES 1:2; ISAIAH 40:6-8; JAMES 4:13-15
Tuesday	MATTHEW 26:39-41; MARK 13:33-37; LUKE 21:36; ROMANS 13:11-12; 1 THESSALONIANS 5:5-6
Wednesday	MARK 8:38; LUKE 9:41; PHILIPPIANS 2:14-16; 2 TIMOTHY 3:1-5
Thursday	LUKE 18:28-30; COLOSSIANS 1:13; HEBREWS 12:28; 1 PETER 1:17-19
Friday	MARK 1:14-15; GALATIANS 4:4-5; HEBREWS 1:1-3
Saturday	EPHESIANS 5:15-17; COLOSSIANS 4:5
Sunday	LUKE 12:54-56

FEATURED SCRIPTURE

Look carefully then how you walk, not as unwise but as wise, making the best use of the time, because the days are evil. Therefore do not be foolish, but understand what the will of the Lord is. —EPHESIANS 5:15-17

3 ACTIVITY OF THE DAY

Monday

Though we will live forever, our families in their present form will soon be gone. What does the transitory nature of this life make you want to do differently in your family while there is still time?

_____

_____

_____

_____

Tuesday

What does it mean, in the words of Jesus and Paul, to "stay [or keep] awake"? Why is this important? Instead of "sleeping," what should we be doing for ourselves and our families?

_____

_____

_____

Wednesday

How did Jesus and Paul describe their generation? How would you describe society today? Why is it important to help your children know what to expect in the world, rather than have false hopes?

_____

_____

_____

_____

Thursday

What is the result of believers having to live in the overlap of two ages—this evil age and the age to come? How can we help our families live as exiles now when our real citizenship is in God's kingdom?

_____

_____

_____

Friday

How blessed are we to live in the "fullness of time," not just looking forward to the Son's coming but being able to read about His visit and personally get to know Him? How does this make living in the corrupt "last days" bearable?

_____

_____

_____

Saturday

Discuss as a family what the apostle Paul meant by exhorting us to "make the best use of the time." How should this command affect our priorities, our choice of activities, our use of "free time"?

_____

_____

_____

_____

Sunday

Memorize this week's featured Bible passage or your favorite portion from one of the other readings.

4 CONCLUSION

The Bible talks about evil growing darker and stronger in the last days. But on a positive note, the apostle Paul reminded the Christians in Rome that "salvation is nearer to us now than when we first believed." Both of these realities should keep us on our toes, ready for all manner of challenges, preparing to suffer for Christ, and making the best use of every day to serve Him. We fail our families if we don't help them realize what time it is and prepare them to be shining lights in the darkness, no matter the cost. And if the cost is high, that's okay, because this life goes by very quickly. Soon we will be rewarded for our faithfulness in the crucible of battle.

5 CLOSING PRAYER

Talk to God alone or together about your family, friends, church, and community, as well as about what He is saying to you today through His Word. Then conclude with this:

> *Father, we are grateful that the trials we have to endure in*
> *this life are nothing compared to the glory ahead. Help us,*
> *as Your children, to be without blemish in the midst of a*
> *crooked and twisted generation. In Jesus's name. Amen.*

Happily Ever After

A rock-solid promise for our future with God

1 OPENING PRAYER

Lord, teach us about, and fill us with, the hope to which You have called us. Then enable us to hold fast to it until You come. Amen.

2 SCRIPTURE READING

Monday	Isaiah 66:22-23; Mark 14:23-25; Romans 8:19-24; Ephesians 1:7-10; 2 Peter 3:11-13
Tuesday	Romans 12:12; 15:13; Ephesians 1:16-21
Wednesday	Titus 2:11-14; Hebrews 3:6; 1 Peter 1:3, 13
Thursday	Isaiah 40:30-31; Ephesians 2:11-13; Hebrews 12:1-2
Friday	Colossians 1:3-5; 2 Thessalonians 2:16-17
Saturday	Hebrews 6:11-12; 10:23; 2 Peter 3:3-4, 8-9; Revelation 2:10, 25-28
Sunday	Revelation 21:1-3

FEATURED SCRIPTURE

Therefore, preparing your minds for action, and being sober-minded, set your hope fully on the grace that will be brought to you at the revelation of Jesus Christ. —1 PETER 1:13

3 ACTIVITY OF THE DAY

Monday

How does it help to know that God didn't give up on His original plan for the earth? That our destiny is not purely "spiritual" but rather a physical life in resurrected bodies on a new earth? Is this news to you?

_____

_____

_____

Tuesday

In past centuries, Christians were wrapped up in joy over the promise of the resurrected life. Why has this certain "hope" somewhat diminished today? How has the distorted notion of a boring, immaterial eternity spoiled the attraction of heaven for many believers?

_____

_____

_____

Wednesday

Is your mind set on the "hope" (a *promise* of God, not something we just wish for) of eternal life, on being with God and your loved ones in a new earth? How will you help family members grasp what's ahead?

_____

_____

_____

Thursday

How does waiting for the fulfillment of God's promises give you strength to get through the day? What would it be like to have no such hope for the future? How do non-Christians live without hope?

_____

_____

_____

Friday

How can being filled with the sure promise of eternal life set us free to love others more deeply? Why does being heavenly-minded make us more useful here on earth, rather than more escapist and uninvolved?

_____

_____

_____

Saturday

What value does God place on our sticking to the hope He promised? On not wavering in our excitement about what He has planned? What can you do for family members who seem to be sluggish in their faith?

_____

_____

_____

_____

Sunday

Memorize this week's featured Bible passage or your favorite portion from one of the other readings.

4 CONCLUSION

Forget playing harps on clouds. And little cherubs flying around. The idea of a spiritual, immaterial heaven came from Greek philosophy, not from the Bible, which promises the resurrection of the *body*. What we look forward to as God's children is a fascinating life on a renewed earth that's even more wonderful than the present one, in bodies that don't cause us pain or wear out. Every fun and creative work (or play) we wanted to do on earth may very well be possible in the future, so there's no need to regret missed opportunities in this life. Places we never got to see? We probably will. Christians from other ages? We'll meet them. Loved ones in the faith whom we're afraid to lose through death? It's only temporary. Best of all, we will see Jesus face-to-face. The Christian who isn't absolutely enthralled with the "blessed hope" is missing a key part of what God intended. Teach these things to your children.

5 CLOSING PRAYER

Talk to God alone or together about your family, friends, church, and community, as well as about what He is saying to you today through His Word. Then conclude with this:

> *Father, according to Your promise, we are waiting for a new heaven and a new earth in which righteousness dwells. Fill us with joy over that prospect and make us people fit to enter Your everlasting kingdom. In Jesus's name. Amen.*

Hear & Obey

*A year-end review of what
God is saying to you*

1 OPENING PRAYER

Lord, give us ears to hear what You are saying through Your Spirit.
Drive home to us the Scriptures You want us to remember always.
Amen.

2 SCRIPTURE READING

Monday	JOHN 10:27-28; HEBREWS 3:13-15
Tuesday	Pick one featured passage from lessons 1–10 and recite or memorize it.
Wednesday	Do the same for lessons 11–20
Thursday	Do the same for lessons 21–30
Friday	Do the same for lessons 31–40
Saturday	Do the same for lessons 41–51
Sunday	MATTHEW 7:24-27

FEATURED SCRIPTURE

*"My sheep hear my voice, and I know them, and they follow me. I give
them eternal life, and they will never perish, and no one will snatch them
out of my hand." —JOHN 10:27-28*

3 ACTIVITY OF THE DAY

Monday

Any general ideas on what God is prompting you to do with your family after going through this devotional guide? What topics would you like to discuss more in a family meeting?

_____

_____

_____

_____

Tuesday

Review the lessons (and your notes) in this guide for weeks 1–10. What biblical commands or ideas seem most important for your family right now? What is God saying to you?

_____

_____

_____

_____

Wednesday

Review the lessons (and your notes) for weeks 11–20. What biblical commands or ideas seem most important for your family right now? What is God saying to you?

_____

_____

_____

_____

Thursday

Review the lessons (and your notes) for weeks 21–30. What biblical commands or ideas seem most important for your family right now? What is God saying to you?

_____

_____

_____

Friday

Review the lessons (and your notes) for weeks 31–40. What biblical commands or ideas seem most important for your family right now? What is God saying to you?

_____

_____

_____

Saturday

Review the lessons (and your notes) for weeks 41–51. What biblical commands or ideas seem most important for your family right now? What is God saying to you?

_____

_____

_____

_____

Sunday

Prepare a fantastic family feast and then use the occasion to share what's uppermost in your mind after this week's review. Be sure everyone has a chance to respond out loud.

4 CONCLUSION

Knowledge is good, but obedience is better. Now that we've studied just about everything God has asked Christians to do with and for one another, it's time to apply what we know. Nowhere are the opportunities for this so great as they are in our own homes. The Christian family is not just one that *hears* what Jesus has to say, but one that *acts* on it. Therein lies the only hope for the family, the church at large, and our lost world.

5 CLOSING PRAYER

Talk to God alone or together about your family, friends, church, and community, as well as about what He is saying to you today through His Word. Then conclude with this:

> *Now to him who is able to keep you from stumbling and to present you blameless before the presence of his glory with great joy, to the only God, our Savior, through Jesus Christ our Lord, be glory, majesty, dominion, and authority, before all time and now and forever. Amen. (Jude 24-25)*

Acknowledgments

Our thanks to counselor Dick Wulf, MSW, for providing an initial outline of pertinent topics, plus many practical ideas for applying the biblical "one anothers" (which he calls the Togethers) to family life. www.ChristiansTogether.org.

About the Author

Ray Seldomridge has been an editor at Focus on the Family for over 30 years and was the founding editor of *Focus on the Family Clubhouse*® and *Focus on the Family Clubhouse Jr.*® magazines. He also worked for World Vision and co-wrote/edited an award-winning children's book with Ruth Bell Graham. Ray holds a bachelor of science degree from the University of California at Santa Barbara and an M.Div. degree from Fuller Theological Seminary. He and his wife, Susan, have three grown sons.